To:

_____

From:

_____

Date:

_____

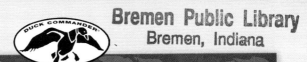

DUCK COMMANDER
Devotions
for Kids

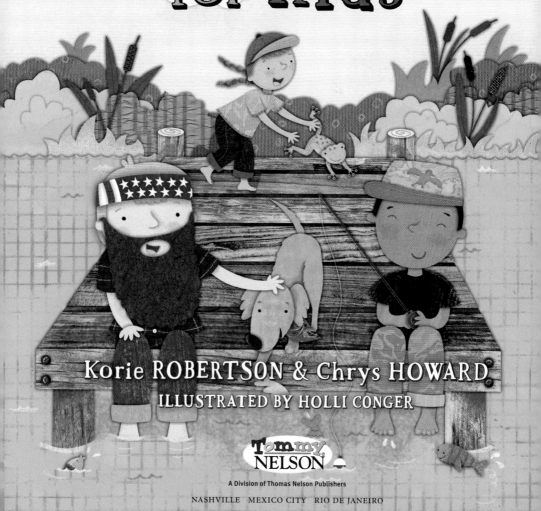

Korie ROBERTSON & Chrys HOWARD
ILLUSTRATED BY HOLLI CONGER

Tommy
NELSON

A Division of Thomas Nelson Publishers

NASHVILLE   MEXICO CITY   RIO DE JANEIRO

Duck Commander Devotions for Kids

© 2015 by Korie Robertson and Chrys Howard

Published in Nashville, Tennessee, by Tommy Nelson. Tommy Nelson is an imprint of Thomas Nelson. Thomas Nelson is a registered trademark of HarperCollins Christian Publishing, Inc.

The Duck Commander logo is used with permission.

Published in association with WME Entertainment, c/o Mel Berger and Margaret Riley King, 1325 Avenue of the Americas, New York, New York 10019.

ISBN-13: 978-0-7180-2249-5

Library of Congress Cataloging-in-Publication Data

Robertson, Korie, 1973- author.
 Duck commander devotions for kids / Korie Robertson and Chrys Howard.
   pages cm
 Summary: "The first devotional for kids by the Robertson family of Duck Dynasty fame! With the Robertson clan's flair for down-home wisdom and their wholesome family values, this devotional reveals the heart and faith of this much-loved family from A&E's hit show Duck Dynasty. The more than 6-million moms, dads, and little ones who are loyal fans of the Duck Dynasty family will love this collection of inspirational messages. Each devotion contains a brief message, an anecdotal story from America's favorite family, a passage from Scripture, a prayer, and a Duck Commander in Action. Not only are the messages motivational, but they are also mixed with the characters' trademark wit and revelations from their personal faith journeys. An ideal companion product for Duck Dynasty fans, outdoor enthusiasts, and those who want to grow in their faith, Duck Commander Devotions for Kids is certain to inspire little ones in their faith journey"-- Provided by publisher.
 Audience: 4-8.
 ISBN 978-0-7180-2249-5 (hardcover) -- ISBN 0-7180-2249-1 (hardcover) 1. Devotional calendars--Juvenile literature. 2. Christian children--Prayers and devotions. 3. Christian life--Biblical teaching--Juvenile literature. 4. Children--Conduct of life--Juvenile literature. I. Howard, Chrys, 1953- author. II. Duck dynasty (Television program) III. Title.
 BV4870.R625 2015
 242.62--dc23
                                2014032006

Printed in the U.S.A.

15 16 17 18 19 RRD 6 5 4

Mfr. RR Donnelley / Crawfordsville, Indiana / January 2015 / 9335491

Contents

DUCK COMMANDER
BUCK COMMANDER

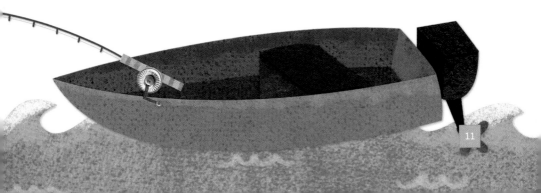

For the Parents . . .

Welcome to *Duck Commander Devotions for Kids*! We are so excited about this book and honored that you have chosen it as a resource for your children. For a few years now, our family has been in the public eye with our TV show, *Duck Dynasty*. If you are a weekly viewer, thank you for supporting us. Our prayer is that the TV show honors God and gives families an opportunity to share their lives as they watch the show together. We also hope the show opens the door for deeper discussions about faith and family.

We are a mother-daughter team, and it has been such fun as we wrote each devotion to recall events that our children, siblings, and parents have gone through. We have tried to make God's words come to life through the use of family stories. These stories are not from the reality show, but from real life. We know that your family has learned many of the same lessons. Of course, your stories might sound a little different from ours (that is, unless you live on a swamp in Louisiana and make duck calls). We hope you enjoy sharing the contents of this book with your children. We love reading to and with our children and know that storytelling is one of the best ways to get a message across to kids. As you read, remember to add your own story. Your kids will love it if you do! Happy reading and studying!

Hugs and Blessings,

Korie and Chrys

For the Children . . .

Welcome to *Duck Commander Devotions for Kids*! We are so happy that you are going to spend some time getting to know God better through this book. We love to read, but we know that reading isn't for everyone so we worked hard to make these messages short, fun, and meaningful. As you read each page, think about your life and the lessons you have already learned. Who knows? One day *you* might write a book!

We know that God has big plans for your life. Our advice is to keep your eyes open to see and your ears ready to hear. That way when God has something important for you to see and hear, you're ready. May God bless you in all you do.

Hugs and Blessings,

Korie and Chrys

Words to Waterproof

Pleasant words are like a honeycomb.
They make a person happy and healthy.
Proverbs 16:24

Poor little Bella was a pacifier addict. Perhaps you were too. A lot of babies love their pacifiers and when it's time to "give it up," they don't want to. But when Korie decided to take her pacifier away, Bella discovered a good thing—without the pacifier in her mouth, she could talk! Soon she was asking for cookies and juice and telling her older brother, Will, "No!" Now Bella had a voice and a choice about how to use it.

A voice means you have words to use, which means you also have words to *choose*. Did you know that your words are super powerful? You have the power to change someone's day just by the words you choose to use. It's true! You can say, "I'm so glad you're my friend," and that person will go through the day feeling happy and encouraged. But if you say something like, "You're no fun. I don't want to play with you," that person will feel sad—all because of what you said. Making the choice to use kind words says a lot about who you are. When you let your words hurt someone, you're making a bad choice. When you use your words to build someone up, that is using your voice to make God happy.

Dear God, I want to bless other people, not hurt them. Please help me use my words to help others. In Jesus' name, Amen.

DUCK Commander in ACTION

Use your words wisely. Refuse to say words that are angry, mean, or hurtful to others. Today is a good day to speak kindly to the kids in your class and in your neighborhood. Think about it like this: there are special sprays that will waterproof your boots so rain will roll right off them. Using kind words helps to waterproof the people you love, causing other unkind words to roll right off them. You will be like a kindness umbrella, covering your friends and brothers and sisters with love!

Work and Be Happy

Hard work always pays off; mere talk puts no bread on the table.
Proverbs 14:23 MSG

Willie loves working outside and loves working with kids, so for ten years he worked at a Christian camp. One thing he learned was that even when you are doing what you love, you still have to work hard. One day the toilets in the girl's village stopped up, and there was no one else to fix them. So Willie did the hard thing (and the yucky thing!)—he fixed the potties and cleaned up the mess so all the campers would have a nice bathroom when they came back to camp.

Did you know that God designed us to work? Even in the garden of Eden, God told Adam and Eve to "work" the garden. Work is a hard thing. We have to use our muscles and our brains to do things like clean a bathroom or sweep the porch or do homework. But it's also the thing that makes us happier people. That doesn't mean

you'll go around smiling the entire time you're sweeping the porch. No. Think about it this way: think of a time when you worked hard at something. Maybe it was a sport you love, like football, or maybe it was a homework assignment and you really gave it your all. You might have been tired when you finished, but you were proud of what you did. It's the way God designed us—working hard gives us a good feeling about ourselves.

Helping your mom clean the kitchen or working with your dad in the yard or doing your homework are all examples of work. Take a few pieces of paper, and write down different jobs you could do. Then take those papers to your mom or dad, and ask them to pick one job for you to do. Your mom or dad will be very surprised and happy, happy, happy when you show them how hard you can work.

God, some days I don't help as much as I should. Please help me to help others so they will see You in me. In His name, Amen.

Speaking Softly Says a Lot

A gentle answer will calm a person's anger. But an unkind word will cause more anger.

Proverbs 15:1

With four boys in the house, Miss Kay was constantly separating her rowdy boys. Each boy felt like it was his job to end an argument. One day, two of the boys were fighting over the oven! Isn't that crazy? At the same time, Willie wanted to make a pizza and Jase wanted to make toast. Their friend was watching the argument and simply said, "You're not being very good examples for God." Both boys stopped what they were doing and ended the fight.

Remember this, yelling louder usually won't end an argument; it just makes the room louder and your mom crazy! But when you are calm, and quietly say what you need to say, things usually get better. The Bible calls this a "gentle" answer. Willie and Jase's friend showed them that a gentle answer really does work. Think about a teacher you might have who talks more softly the louder the kids get. She will get the room to be quieter by being quiet herself. That's a smart teacher. There is a funny saying that goes, "Even a fish wouldn't get into trouble if he kept his mouth shut."

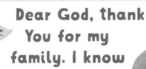

Dear God, thank You for my family. I know I need to be more patient sometimes. Help me to speak kindly and lovingly to my brothers and sisters. In Jesus' name, Amen.

DUCK Commander in ACTION

All brothers and sisters argue sometimes. But it's important to remember that our families are the people who will love us for our whole lives. If you see yourself ready to argue with your brother or sister, stop and count to ten. After you have reached ten, if you are still angry, start counting again. Counting takes your attention away from the problem, and you will learn to think before you speak.

God's Love Is an Open Door

Whoever does not love does not
know God, because God is love.
1 John 4:8

Missy and her children are the singers in the Robertson family. (Uncle Si wins the prize for being the **LOUDEST** singer. It could wake a hibernating bear from his winter-long sleep!) One of our favorite songs is simply called "Love One Another." It's a great song because it talks about love being from God.

Love is a word that can mean many things. Sometimes we say we love ice cream or we love a pet or we love our parents. Each of those types of love is different. We really don't love our parents in the same way we love ice cream, do we?

God has blessed us with so many things to love, and because we are human, we might love something one day and something else another day! But God's love for us will never change. The

Bible tells us His love endures forever! How long is forever? Well, it's like saying the word *on* over and over and never stopping. Like this: on and on and on and on and on and on and on. Do you get it? Forever doesn't have an ending. It keeps on going. It's great to know that God's love for us will keep on going too.

Dear God, thank You for loving me so much that You sent Your only Son to die for me. Thank You for always being there for me. In Jesus' name, Amen.

DUCK Commander in ACTION

Frozen was a very popular movie in 2014. Everyone was singing the songs, and they were great songs! One of the Robertson favorites was "Love Is an Open Door." The song says that life can be so much more with love. But life can be even MORE with God's love. Here's a fun activity for you to do. Draw a heart on a piece of paper. Next, decorate the heart with the things you love. You can either write them with a marker or cut them out of a magazine and glue them on. Then share what you made with your family.

Thank You

Praise the Lord. Give thanks to the LORD, for
he is good; his love endures forever.

Psalm 106:1 NIV

When Phil and Miss Kay were first married, they didn't have much money for food, but God always provided for them with fresh fish and deer meat. Phil didn't know God and didn't understand that God was taking care of them. He wasn't thankful for the food they had to eat. One day a special friend told Phil about God, and Phil began to read his Bible. He learned that God loves and takes care of His people. That was many years ago. Now Phil always prays before every meal, showing his children and grandchildren that he knows that God has provided for them.

Sometimes we forget to thank God for all the blessings in our lives. When you do something nice for someone, it's good to hear them say "thank you." God also loves to hear us say "thank You." How do we tell God we're thankful? We can thank Him by praying to Him or singing a song or reading His words in the Bible. These are all great ways to tell God that you love Him and you know He is taking care of you.

Father in heaven, thank You for everything! I know that all good things come from You, so thank You for all that You have given me. In His name, Amen.

DUCK Commander in ACTION

It only takes a few seconds to be thankful. It's only two simple words—*thank* and *you*—but they mean so much. Today is a great day to thank God for the things He has blessed you with. Take out a piece of paper, and write down some of those things. You might be thankful for yummy food to eat or for a family who loves you.

Then put that list on your refrigerator or on the bathroom mirror in your room. That way you will be reminded every day to thank God.

The Good Book

*Follow God's example, therefore,
as dearly loved children.*

Ephesians 5:1 NIV

Miss Kay loves to cook. In fact, she has her own cookbook called *Miss Kay's Duck Commander Kitchen*! When she decides to make a cake, she has to follow the instructions carefully so that she can make the cake exactly right. If you have ever tried to make a cake, you had to do the same thing—or else it might have exploded in the oven! Cookbooks are good to have because someone has already tested the recipes and written them down for us to follow.

Did you know that God gave us an instruction book too? It's called the Bible. The Bible is our guide to getting to heaven, and it gives us instructions on how to live a good life while on earth. If we will read our Bibles every day, we will learn more about God and His plan for our lives. The Bible has instructions for how to treat your brothers and sisters, how to be a good son or daughter, and how to treat your neighbors. If you like to cook, then a cookbook is very important. If you want to live for God, the most important book is His book, the Bible.

Lord, I want to know more about You. Thank You for the Bible so I can learn Your will for me. Give me ears to hear and eyes to see. In Jesus' name, Amen.

DUCK Commander in ACTION

First read this verse from James 1:19–20: "My dear brothers and sisters, take note of this: Everyone should be quick to listen, slow to speak and slow to become angry, because human anger does not produce the righteousness that God desires" (NIV). Next, circle the words in this verse that tell you a way to act. (Hint: you should have circled "quick to listen," "slow to speak," and "slow to become angry.") These are all important lessons. Just think about all the great ways you'll learn to live a better life when you read your Bible!

Talk About Jesus

I praise your greatness, my
God the King. I will praise
you forever and ever.

Psalm 145:1 NCV

One time Willie went on a mission trip to another country. In this country, the people spoke Spanish. Willie couldn't speak Spanish, so someone had to translate what he said to the people. He was there to tell them how much God loves them and how to live for God and to make Him number one in their lives. But one day the interpreter got confused. Instead of saying Willie's words in Spanish, he just repeated them in English. Soon everyone was laughing because no one could understand the interpreter *or* Willie!

Even though no one could understand him, Willie was saying great things about God. He was praising God by talking about Him. And he was doing what the Bible commands: to tell others about Jesus. When we talk about God to other people, it shows God that He is important to us. It's kind of like when you like a certain movie and want others to see it. You tell your friends and family all about it. Some people may not want to hear about it, but you tell them anyway. They might change their minds and go see the movie. The same could be true of your words about God. Some people may not want to hear, but if you tell them about how much He loves them and wants to be their friend, they might start to listen and ask questions. And you'll be there to answer them!

Dear Father, I want to share my love for You with others. Help me to use my words to lead others to You. In His name, Amen.

DUCK Commander in ACTION

Someone really close to you may never have heard about Jesus. You don't have to sound like a grown-up to tell a friend about Jesus. You don't even have to go to a foreign country like Willie did. You just have to be willing to say how much you love God and what a good friend He is. One good way to share about God's love is to make a bookmark for your friends. You can just cut out strips of paper and write your favorite verse on them. Maybe you'll even add some of your own artwork! Then pass out the bookmarks to your friends. Every time they use them, they will be reminded that God loves them.

The Bible, Our Powerful Sword

God's word is alive and working.
It is sharper than a sword
sharpened on both sides.
Hebrews 4:12

What is your favorite drink? Have you ever had iced tea? In the South, people drink iced tea to keep cool on hot summer days. But Uncle Si drinks iced tea *every day*—even in the winter! He has a special cup his mother sent him when he was a soldier fighting a war in another country. That cup reminded him of his family back home, so he kept it close.

If you see Uncle Si today, you'll see that same iced tea cup in his hand.

Do you have something special like a stuffed animal or a blanket that you like to keep close? Blankets and stuffed animals can also remind us of our family and help us feel safe.

Uncle Si keeps something else close to him: his Bible. He loves iced tea and his tea cup, but he loves his Bible *even more*. He knows that the Bible has God's words written in it, and those words are as powerful as a very sharp sword. Imagine if you were in a battle, but you forgot your sword! Wow! That would make the battle very hard to win. It's the same way with the Bible. If you don't keep it close, you won't have it as you fight the battles of life. God's Word is our weapon against Satan. When we have the words of the Bible in our heart, Satan can't come in!

Dear God, thank You for Your love and protection. And thank You for Your Word, the Bible. When I need Your words, I know they are there for me. In Jesus' name, Amen.

DUCK Commander in ACTION

The Bible compares God's words to a powerful sword. That's because God's words can help you fight against Satan, just like a sword would help you fight an enemy in battle. How do God's words help you fight? Say Psalm 18:1—"I love you, Lord. You are my strength"—out loud ten times. Each time you say it, you are telling Satan that *God* is your strength. When you need God's help, like if someone is being mean to you or a friend, this verse will help you. An adult can help you cut out a sword from construction paper. Write this verse on the sword.

Treasures in Heaven

"So store your treasure in heaven. The treasures in heaven cannot be destroyed by moths or rust. And thieves cannot break in and steal that treasure."

Matthew 7:20

John Luke is always looking for an adventure. He loves to find treasures, and he saves them in special places. One time when he was at the beach, he found a huge shell. He thought he had found the best shell ever! He put the shell in his pocket, but later forgot about it. Then his cousins wanted him to go play in the waves. The waves knocked John Luke down, and he fell right on that shell in this pocket. The shell cut him, and he had to put on a bandage so he could go outside and play again.

The Bible tells us to store our treasures in heaven. *To store* means to save or keep. Does that mean we should send our seashells or special rocks up to heaven? That might be a better place to keep them than your pocket, but God probably has plenty of special shells and pretty rocks in heaven already! Keeping our treasures in heaven means we should count our heavenly things as our most valuable treasures—things like the love of our family or our friends at church. These are our *real* treasures, and these are the things we should spend time and energy on. What are some of the real treasures you could be saving up for in heaven?

Dear God, thank You for all the treasures You have given me. Help me to always be thankful and to treat my treasures as special. In His name, Amen.

Today's a great day for a treasure hunt! Get a paper sack and go outside. Find these things: a rock, three leaves, two blades of grass, a small stick, and a flower. It's fun to look for treasures, and these are all things God made for us to enjoy. But remember, God's best treasures are inside your home: your mom, dad, brothers, and sisters. You can't put them in a sack, but you can keep their love for you in your heart.

Be YOU!

Know that the Lord is God. He made
us and we belong to him. We are his
people, the sheep he tends.
Psalm 100:3

When Sadie was just a toddler, her dad, Willie, nicknamed her "The Original." To be original means to be different from anything else, and Sadie was always doing something that was different. Now that Sadie is older, she loves to tell people that we are all originals. She says God created you to be you, and Sadie to be Sadie, and everyone else to be who they are.

Did you know that there are millions of snowflakes? It's true! Every year God creates millions of snowflakes, but each snowflake is an original. No two snowflakes are alike. That is true of people too. Even if you have a twin who looks like you, you are still different. It's pretty amazing how God can keep creating babies who are different! Sometimes we look around and want to be like someone else. Maybe we think they are cooler or prettier or smarter or taller. But remember, you are as special as a snowflake! Be happy with who you are. Be proud of the color of your eyes and the way you talk, because God created you to be special and one-of-a-kind. Be confident about who you are, and work on being the best YOU that you can be!

Dear God, thank You for making me just as I am. Help me to use my talents to serve You better and to be happy with who I am. In Jesus' name, Amen.

DUCK Commander in ACTION

Look around at your family. You will see that everyone has some things that are alike and some things that are different. Draw a line down the middle of a piece of paper. On the top of the paper, write *alike* and *different*. Now see if you can write down five things about yourself that are like your family members and five things that are different.

A Clean Heart

Create in me a pure heart, God, and
make my spirit right again.
Psalm 51:10 NCV

Korie loves art and was an art teacher at a summer camp for many years. She likes for her students to create their own projects from scratch. That means you don't have a guide; you have to use your own imagination. Korie would give the kids a piece of paper, a paintbrush, and some paint. Then she would say something like, "Create a painting about your best day last summer." Then the students would create their own masterpieces.

Some other words for *create* are *build*, *make*, and *form*. Our verse for today was written a long time ago by King David after he had disappointed God. He asked God to *create* a pure or clean heart in him. How would someone make a clean heart? You can't use a paintbrush and paint to do it. That would be a mess! You can't even use crayons or markers. King David was talking about a different kind of creation, like when we watch a flower bloom or a tree grow new leaves. These are things that no one on earth can create—not even Korie! Only God can make those powerful creations. King David wanted God's help so that he would keep his eyes on God and not let anyone (or his own bad choices) lead him to do the wrong thing. When we do something wrong, God wants us to ask for forgiveness and to stop doing that wrong thing. That's how we get a clean heart.

Dear Lord, thank You for loving me and for forgiving me. Help me to forgive others the way You forgive me. In His name, Amen.

We usually clean at least one thing every day. Can you think of some of the things you or your parents clean? How about the dishes? Your hair? The car? Isn't it nice to have these things clean? It makes you feel good to have freshly washed hair or a sparkling car. Did you know that God cleans something every day too? He cleans our hearts by showing us His love and forgiveness. Draw a heart on a piece of paper, and write these words on it: *Thank You, God, for a clean heart.*

Buried for Us

And this was the most important: . . . that he was buried and was raised to life on the third day as the Scriptures say.

1 Corinthians 15:3

The Robertson family loves to vacation at the beach. The men play golf, while the women and kids spend their days enjoying the sun and playing in the waves. One year, everyone decided to bury Little Will in the sand. Will's a big guy, so it was a lot of work and took a long time, but soon all you could see of Will was his face! Everyone thought he looked so funny, and they took lots of pictures. After that, Will started kicking his way out of the sand and got up and ran to the water.

There's a very important story in the Bible about another person who was buried: Jesus Christ. He died on a cross to save us from our sins, and then He was buried. The Bible tells us that He was buried for three whole days before something amazing happened: He rose from the

dead! He didn't have to kick or fight His way out of the tomb, but we do know His friends and family were surprised to see Him. They were so sad He had died and didn't think they'd see Him again. But God sent Jesus back to show the world that He is more powerful than death.

Dear God, thank You for sending Your Son, Jesus, to earth and for letting Him die and be buried for our sins and then rise from the dead! Help me to always remember the sacrifice You made for us. In Jesus' name, Amen.

To be buried means to be put in the ground and covered up with dirt. Pirates used to bury their treasure to keep it away from other pirates. Some people bury a time capsule (a box or other container filled with things about them and the time when they are living). Look around your house for things that describe you: a movie poster, a page out of a magazine, a toy, a piece of candy, your favorite book, or anything else you like. Put them in a jar, and bury it in your yard. You might want to write a letter about who you are too. It will be a fun surprise for someone to uncover many years from now.

Living in Love

It is good and pleasant when God's
people live together in peace!
Psalm 133:1

Many people don't know that all of the Robertson family—except Phil and Miss Kay—live on the same street. It's fun for all the cousins to live close to each other, and on most afternoons they are either jumping on a trampoline or turning flips in someone's yard. It's also fun when they bring friends over to the neighborhood.

Did you know that your family and friends help you learn how to be a good person? They help you learn how to treat people and what words to use to make others happy.

Think about it like this: if you lived on an island with no friends or family, you could act any way you wanted. You could talk mean; you could throw things; you could even scream at the top of your lungs! You would also be alone . . . but when you live with

others, you have to speak kindly, take care of your things, and not yell or scream. This is good training for all the years to come. God is happy with us when we treat others kindly. He created all people, and He wants everyone to get along.

DUCK Commander in ACTION

Cut a piece of construction paper into strips. On each strip write the name of a different family member or friend. Use glue or tape to make a chain out of the strips. That chain will remind you that family and friends are important links in your chain of life. As you link each chain together, say a prayer for that person.

Dear God, thank You for my family and friends. I want to treat them with love and kindness. In Your name, Amen.

Fishing for Men

"Come, follow me," Jesus said, "and I
will send you out to fish for people."
Matthew 4:19 NIV

Phil loves to fish. When he was a young man, his job was fishing. He would fish all day long and then take his fish to market and sell them. Then he would use the money he made to buy other things his family needed. Fishing was very important to Phil and his family. All of his sons learned how to fish and how to keep the fish fresh and cold until they got it to market.

Phil still fishes, but he doesn't have to sell his fish to make money anymore. He fishes these days to have a good fish fry with his family and friends. Phil does a different kind of fishing now—he fishes for people. It's something God tells all of us to do, but what does it mean to "fish for people"? It doesn't mean to catch a man with a fishing pole! That would be silly. It means that God wants us to tell other people about the Jesus we know. It's important to remember that everyone needs to hear about God and His love for us. It doesn't matter how old you are or how much you know. There will always be someone who needs to hear what you know about Jesus. This is a different kind of fishing, but you can do it!

Lord, I want to learn how to fish for people and tell them about You and Your love. Please help me to be patient and brave. In Jesus' name, Amen.

Fishing is so much fun, but you really have to be patient. You might sit out by the lake for *an hour* before you catch a fish. Right now, everyone you know might already go to church, but if you're patient, God will put people in your life who have never heard about Jesus. Look around your school or your neighborhood, and see if there is someone who needs to hear about God. Ask him to come to church with you. That's how you will become a fisher of men.

Making Good Choices

I am writing this not to shame you but
to warn you as my dear children.
1 Corinthians 4:14 NIV

One day, John Luke decided to buy a sailboat. He had never sailed, but he thought it seemed easy enough. It had stormed the night before his first sailing trip, and the water was very rough. His parents told him that they weren't sure it was a safe time to try sailing, but John Luke was eager to take the boat out. He tried to raise the sails as the wind whipped around him, but he wasn't strong enough to raise them in that wind. After a while, John Luke decided to pay attention to the warning signs: the strong wind, the big waves, and his mom and dad's concerns.

Sometimes you might want to do something, but warning signs are telling you it's not a good idea. Maybe you want to watch a certain TV show or do a certain activity with friends, but you're not sure if it's okay. It's important to listen to warning signs because they will keep us safe and protect us from going through some hard times. If John Luke hadn't ultimately listened to his parents and the weather report, he could have been in danger. The waves could have flipped his boat, or the wind could have torn the new sail. God has given us a brain to make wise decisions. Be smart. Use your brain to make good choices. Use your ears to listen to your parents or a teacher. They love you and will help you make right choices.

Dear God, thank You for blessing me with a brain that I can use to make good decisions. Help me to always stop, look, and listen before I do things. In Jesus' name, Amen.

DUCK Commander in ACTION

Making good choices depends on *you*! Every day you will be given opportunities to make good decisions. For instance, you might need to decide to ignore your little brother or sister who is bothering you, or you might need to decide to pick up the toys in your room. You have a lot of power over your behavior! The next time you are faced with a decision, try this: stop, look, and listen. **STOP** what you are doing, **LOOK** at the situation, and **LISTEN** if someone older and wiser is there to help you. That way, you will make good choices.

I Forgive You

Forgive each other because
the Lord forgave you.
Colossians 3:13

Have you ever heard the expression "blood is thicker than water"? It means that family will always stand up for one another. Brothers and sisters seem to fight with each other at home, but when other kids start to pick on one of them, a good brother or sister will come to the rescue. This is how it should be. But sometimes our brothers or sisters can really make us mad. When Jeptha was younger, the other brothers picked on him because he was the youngest. Jeptha has had to forgive them—even when it's hard! They are his family, and they stick together. And forgiveness is something God tells us to do.

Forgiveness really isn't a feeling; it's a decision. When you forgive someone, you aren't saying what the person did is okay; you are saying you have decided to not hold it against that person. It takes a very special kind of love and courage to forgive. Some might think that forgiving someone means you're weak, but the opposite is true. You are very brave and very strong when you choose to forgive. God sent His Son, Jesus, to die for us. With His blood, He forgave us when we were still sinners. It's by His example and His gift to us that we can forgive others.

DUCK Commander in ACTION

Think of a time when someone hurt your feelings, and write it down on a piece of paper. Go bury that piece of paper in the yard. You are telling yourself that you are letting it go. Remember, forgiveness is all about what *you* do. The other person might not even apologize. Forgiveness is God's command, and it is for your heart, not for the other person.

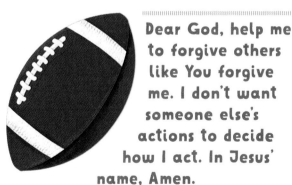

Dear God, help me to forgive others like You forgive me. I don't want someone else's actions to decide how I act. In Jesus' name, Amen.

God Is *Not* Surprised

God is greater than our hearts,
and he knows everything.

1 John 3:20

John Luke loves to surprise people. One summer, John Luke caught a snake and decided to surprise Sadie with it. He put it in a box and wrapped it up like a present. When Sadie opened the box and saw the snake, she screamed. John Luke's surprise worked! But Sadie wasn't very happy. Another time, John Luke surprised his grandmother with a beautiful bouquet of flowers he had made out of pipe cleaners. He worked really hard on that surprise, and she loved it. Surprises are usually fun, aren't they? We love to be surprised at Christmas or on our birthday with special gifts. But it's even more fun on days when you aren't expecting a surprise, like when you come home from school and your mom has made cookies or when your dad goes on a trip and brings home a treat. Those surprises are the best!

Think about this: God loves to surprise His children but He can never be surprised.

Surprises can only work when you don't know what is going to happen. God knows and sees everything, so He cannot be surprised. We should be very thankful that God is always awake, always alert, and always there to love, guide, and protect us. Nothing surprises Him! So when you're having a bad day, God is not surprised. When you're sick, God is not surprised. He already knows what you're going through and is ready to help you.

DUCK Commander in ACTION

We know that God is not surprised, but we also know that people love to be surprised. Today would be a good day to surprise your mom with something special. Write a note to her or pick her a flower. Then leave it on her bed for her to discover later. This is a surprise that will make her feel very special.

God, I love surprises! But I also love that You are never surprised because You already know what is going to happen. Thank You for loving and protecting me. In Your name, Amen.

Talk to God

Pray with all kinds of prayers, and
ask for everything you need.
Ephesians 6:9

Prayer is a gift God gives each of us. Prayer is simply talking to God, just like you would talk to your friends or your parents. Talking to God is one way we get closer to Him. If you have a friend, but you never talk to that friend, you won't be friends for very long. God wants us to talk to Him, so we can get to know each other better. A prayer can be long or short—length and fancy words don't matter. What matters is that you talk to God.

Miss Kay has lots of dogs. She loves her dogs so much. You might have a dog that you love too. Miss Kay talks to her dogs. She tells them she loves them, and she calls them when she has food for them. You might hear her on the TV show hollering, "Bo Bo!" or "Jessi!" When she yells their names, the dogs always come running. But what if Miss Kay spent all her time talking to her dogs and no time talking to God? God would be sad, and Miss Kay would miss out on getting to know God better. Miss Kay makes sure she spends time with God in prayer. That's how she calls to God. When she says, "Dear God," God is there, ready to talk. God is always here and always hears us—our heavenly Father who loves to hear His name called.

Dear God, thank You for always being ready to listen to my prayers. I want to talk to You. Help me to remember to pray about things that matter to me and others. In His name, Amen.

DUCK Commander in ACTION

You're never too young to start a prayer list. A prayer list is a list of things you want to remember to pray about. Maybe you know someone who is sick or hurt. You can put that person on your prayer list. Take a piece of paper, and write numbers down the side. Then start writing things you need to pray for and are thankful for. Soon you will have a long prayer list. Keep it beside your bed, and every night you can talk to God before you shut off the light.

Brothers Helping Brothers

Love each other like brothers and sisters.
Give your brothers and sisters more
honor than you want for yourselves.
Romans 12:10

Phil and Uncle Si are brothers. They do everything together. They hunt together. They take naps at the same time. They watch The Weather Channel together. They are best friends. Miss Kay says Uncle Si was with them when she and Phil went on their first date. Now that's a close brother! But Uncle Si isn't Phil's only brother. Phil has three more—Jimmy Frank, Tommy, and Harold! Having a brother or sister means you will always have someone to play with and someone to talk to—and someone to look out for you if you need help. Phil and his brothers are glad they are brothers and know they can always count on each other. When Phil was in college, he and his brother Tommy would fish together so they would have food for supper. They worked together to make sure they had food.

The Bible talks about another kind of brother: your friends in Jesus, who are your "brothers" too. They aren't related to you by being in your family, but they are in the family of God. That's even better! All the boys and girls who love God and follow Him are your brothers and sisters. Just like Phil and his brothers are there for each other, you and your brothers and sisters in Jesus should always be ready to help each other out. The Bible tells us that someone who takes care of his brothers and sisters shows others that he has God's love in his heart.

Dear God, thank You for the family I live with and for my family in Christ. Help me remember to help them when they need me. In Jesus' name, Amen.

DUCK Commander in ACTION

Your mom probably has some magazines around the house. Ask if you can look through them to find pictures of brothers and sisters—having fun together, helping one another, and laughing. When you find one you like, cut it out and tape it to your mirror. When you look at that picture, you'll remember what it means to be a good brother or sister to all of God's family.

Everyone Is Important

If each part of the body were the same part, there would be no body. But truly God put the parts in the body as he wanted them. He made a place for each one of them.

1 Corinthians 12:18–19

Have you ever seen a duck call? Have you ever *blown* a duck call? A duck call isn't very big, but it can make a really **BIG** sound. Uncle Si has been the reed maker for the duck calls for many years. The reed is a very important part of a duck call. (Uncle Si thinks it's the most important part.) If a duck call didn't have a reed, it wouldn't sound like a duck! But the reed isn't the only important part. Without the wedge, the soundboard, and the end piece, the call

wouldn't work at all; it wouldn't sound like a duck. All the parts are equally important.

It probably doesn't surprise you that *you* are more important than any part of a duck call. It's true! You were made by God—the ultimate Creator—and no one else on earth is just like you. Even if you have a twin, that twin is different in some way. And like every part of a duck call, every part of God's family is important. We all have different jobs to do because God made us all different. Some people are good singers, some are good speakers, others can play a musical instrument, some learn quickly in school, and others make friends easily. It's so cool that God knows how to create us all so differently! Be happy that God made you just like you are, and use the talents He gave you to serve Him better.

DUCK
Commander
in ACTION

Here's a fun thing you can do today. Ask your mom if you can borrow her cell phone. Go to each member of your family, and take a picture of them doing what they are talented in doing. Maybe you have a sister who likes to sing. Take her picture singing. Perhaps your dad can draw. Take a picture of him drawing. You will learn a lot about your family and see how God has blessed each one of them.

Lord, thank You for making me *me*! I want to keep learning about the talents You gave me. Help me to use them in the right way. In His name, Amen.

Taming Your Tongue

People can tame all kinds of animals,
birds, reptiles, and fish, but no one
can tame the tongue. It is restless
and evil, full of deadly poison.

James 3:7-8 NLT

Many people think that alligators come right up to the houses in Louisiana, where the Robertsons live, but that isn't true. In fact, it's rare to see an alligator. But one day an alligator *did* get in the small pond behind Willie's house. It was very scary for a while until a friend came out to catch it. This friend knew all about alligators and exactly how to catch him without getting hurt. He told the Robertson family to meet him at the pond at midnight. Everyone gathered around the pond and looked and looked for the alligator. Soon his eyes peered up out of the water. Then the alligator hunter waded into the water and, very quickly, grabbed the alligator behind his jaws and carefully carried him to land. John Luke was waiting on the side of the pond with tape and wrapped the tape tightly around the gator's mouth, just like the hunter told him to. Once everyone knew the alligator couldn't bite them, they were able to come close to pet it (but we definitely

wouldn't have done that without a professional there to make sure everyone was safe!).

As strong as that alligator was, the Bible tells us that people—even you!—have a body part that is even stronger. What could be stronger than an alligator? Would you believe that your tongue is stronger? Yes, the Bible says your tongue is more powerful than lots of big animals! That's because an animal can be caught and have tape wrapped around its mouth, but our tongues cannot be caught. Our tongues are free to say and do whatever we allow—including saying mean or unkind things or even lying. But we can work to make good choices with our tongues. We can choose to use our tongues to say kind words, to pray to God, and to share about His goodness. God is very happy when we tame our tongues and use them for good.

DUCK Commander in ACTION

You have probably never thought about how powerful or strong your tongue is and how hard it is to control it. Time yourself, and see if you can stop talking for one hour. Tell your mom and dad what you are doing so they will help you. It might be harder than you think to keep your tongue quiet, but you can do it!

Dear God, thank You for giving me a tongue to use. Please help me to control it and to say only things that help others and You. In Jesus' name, Amen.

Find Your Talents

"Bring to me all the people
who are mine. I made
them for my glory."
Isaiah 43:7

Some of us are really good at sports. Some are good at art. Others are good at reading. What are you good at? Just because we're good at one thing doesn't mean we shouldn't try another thing. John Luke loves to try to new things, even if he's not very good at them. Each year at school he tries a new activity. One year he played football. The next year he played baseball. And then he decided to try golf. He wasn't the best at any of these, but he always learned something just by trying, and he had fun too.

One year John Luke decided to try art, and guess what? He discovered he likes it and is good at it! God has given you talents too. You might have to try several activities before you know exactly what your talents are.

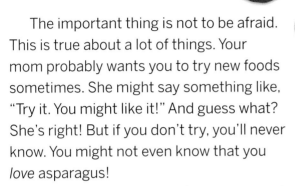

The important thing is not to be afraid. This is true about a lot of things. Your mom probably wants you to try new foods sometimes. She might say something like, "Try it. You might like it!" And guess what? She's right! But if you don't try, you'll never know. You might not even know that you *love* asparagus!

Think about trying new things as a way to challenge yourself and to grow. Remember that God created you and your talents. He wants you to discover those talents and then use them to show others about Him.

Dear God, thank You for making me special! I will be listening and watching to see what talents You have given me and how I can use them for You. In Jesus' name, Amen.

Shout to the Lord

Everything on earth, shout with joy to God!
Psalm 66:1

Summer camp is a big part of the Robertsons' summer plans. Each summer, we go to a camp called Camp Ch-Yo-Ca. We have lots of fun playing games like volleyball and basketball. But one of the most popular games at camp is called Nitty-Gritty. The leader calls out a certain item or activity and each team has to either find it or perform it. Sometimes the item might be something like a pine cone, or it could be the girl with the longest hair. Everyone loves the loudest scream contest too! Each team has to send the loudest screamer to the center of the room, and they have a scream-off. It gets *very* loud! Think about a football or basketball game where everyone is cheering and yelling. That gets loud too, doesn't it? Your mom would probably complain if you yelled at home like you do at a ballgame or at a screaming contest.

One year at camp, one of the Bible teachers told the campers it was time to cheer and yell for God. The teacher explained that

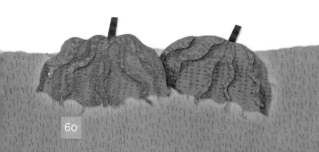

God is better than any ballgame and deserves to hear us shouting about Him and His love and goodness. So everyone gathered around the campfire and looked up to the sky and cheered as loud as they could. It was a loud, happy noise for God!

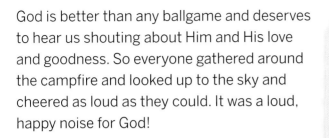

Dear God, I want to shout with joy about You! I want the world to know that I love You. Help me not to be afraid to shout about You. In His name, Amen.

DUCK Commander in ACTION

Your mom might ask you to do *this* activity outside, but once you explain the idea, she will be happy. Say the verse Psalm 66:1 out loud: "Everything on earth, shout with joy to God!" Then start cheering and yelling for God like you would at a ballgame or after you watch a performance you like. This will make God very happy!

Be Strong and Brave

"Remember that I commanded you to be strong and brave. So don't be afraid. The Lord your God will be with you everywhere you go."

Joshua 1:9

When Sadie was just twelve years old, she was asked to play on a basketball team in Austria. She would have to leave her family and travel on an airplane to another country all by herself. Sadie wasn't sure she could do this. Then she remembered that God created her and loves her, and He also promised to protect her. So she went to Austria.

While Sadie was there, she met some girls who did not know God. She wasn't sure she could be brave enough to tell them about Him. But again, she remembered God's promise to protect her. She told the girls all about how much she loves Jesus and that she will follow Him all her life.

Standing strong and being brave can be hard to do. When you see a person treating someone in a bad way, you might need to be brave to stand up to them. Or if you are asked to read a Scripture or say a prayer out loud, you may need some courage to do it. The Bible tells us that when we don't feel strong, God will be there to help us. God loves to be our sword and our shield whenever we need Him.

Dear God, thank You for always being here for me. Help me to be brave and strong when I am faced with a trial or with a big job. In Jesus' name, Amen.

DUCK Commander in ACTION

The word *strong* can mean lots of things. It could mean using your muscles in your arms and legs to be strong. It could also mean how you use your words. When you use your words for good, you are being a strong leader for others who need to see Jesus. Write the word S-T-R-O-N-G on a piece of paper. For each letter, write another word that would go with being strong. For example, *S* could mean "support" and *T* could be "try" and *R* could mean "real." Now you work on O, N, and G.

Grow in Faith

We hope that your faith will continue to grow.
2 Corinthians 10:15

Will was only ten months old when his sister, Bella, was born. Because they were so close in age, they did many things together. Instead of saying they were little troublemakers, Korie would say they were very *busy*. Every day, Korie would find Will and Bella getting into things around the house. She might find them pouring out a box of cereal or climbing through a window. Maybe you have a little brother or sister you have to watch so he or she doesn't do something crazy or maybe even get hurt! Or maybe *you* were "busy" like Will and Bella.

Now that Will and Bella are older, they know how to behave. That's true for all of us. As we get older, we learn that dumping out a box of cereal isn't a smart decision and that if we climb out a window we might get hurt! That's called *growing up*. You would laugh if you saw your mom and dad doing the things a baby or a toddler does. That would be silly! As we grow up, we learn to make better decisions and to make good choices.

The Bible talks about another way to grow up. It's called

growing in faith. Growing in faith means learning more and more about Jesus. With each new thing we learn about Him, we grow, and our faith gets stronger. It's like when you turn on the faucet at your house and water pours out. You trust that the water will be there. When your faith gets stronger, it's like turning on a faucet—you can trust that God will be there every time. When we read the Bible and learn about God and what He does, our faith grows. We learn to trust Him and to believe that His words are true and that He will always be there. And our faith keeps growing and growing!

God, I want to grow to be more like You. Help me to study and to understand what You are saying to me. Help me to grow strong in You! In Jesus' name, Amen.

DUCK Commander in ACTION

It's really cool how everything God created grows. Flowers, trees, animals, and people— we all grow! Ask your mom to let you plant a special flower or tree to be your "faith tree." Every time you water it and check on it, let it remind you that you should be growing too. To grow in your faith, you will need to read your Bible and pray and sing praise songs. And then you will grow and *grow* and *GROW* closer to God.

Copy This!

Remember your leaders. They
taught God's message to you.
Remember how they lived and
died, and copy their faith.
Hebrews 13:7

Sadie is the family imitator. Do you know what an imitator is? That's a big word for someone who tries to talk and act like someone else. Sadie loves to talk and act just like her teachers or her basketball coach or one of her friends! Everyone in the family laughs when she does this because she's very good at it.

Another word for imitating is *copying*. If you wanted to copy someone's drawing, you would study it closely and then try to draw it exactly as you saw it. The Bible talks about copying too. It even talks about copying people just like Sadie does. To copy or imitate a person, you would have to look at him or her really closely, just like a drawing you were trying to copy. Sadie likes to be funny with some of her imitations, like saying, "Hey, Jack!" to imitate Uncle Si, but she knows it's more important to copy the godly things her grandparents and parents do. She goes to church every Sunday like her Papaw Phil does and memorizes Scriptures like her Mamaw Howard, and she shares about Jesus like all her uncles do. This is the best kind of copying! Copying for Jesus!

DUCK Commander in ACTION

Being able to copy something can be harder than it looks. Ask your mom or a friend to draw a picture of a tree, and then try to draw it just like they drew it. Write the words of Hebrews 13:7 under your picture to remind you to copy the good things your family members have done.

Lord, help me to look at others and see the good things in them that I need to put in my life. Thank You for giving me great examples to follow. In His name, Amen.

Laugh Every Day

A happy heart is like good medicine.
Proverbs 17:22

Rebecca is Korie and Willie's oldest daughter, but she didn't become part of the family until she was sixteen. She came to America to go to school and learn about another country. Rebecca is from Taiwan. Everything is different in Taiwan. They eat different food, wear different clothes, and speak a different language. Rebecca had to learn how to speak English when she came to America. It was hard for her, but she worked really hard, and soon she could say anything she wanted to say.

Have you ever heard someone tell a joke that you didn't understand? Rebecca wanted to learn to speak English so she could laugh at the family jokes. All of the Robertsons are funny, but if you can't understand what they are saying, it's not funny at all. Now that Rebecca can speak English, she gets to laugh with her family every day. God created us to laugh. Laughter is a good thing! Look for something to laugh at every day. Be thankful when you can understand a joke and be thankful that you can laugh.

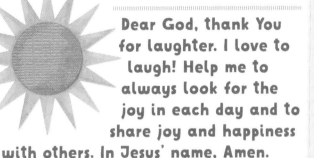

Dear God, thank You for laughter. I love to laugh! Help me to always look for the joy in each day and to share joy and happiness with others. In Jesus' name, Amen.

DUCK Commander in ACTION

Telling jokes is one way to get people to laugh, but it's not the only way. Sometimes we can make a funny face or just say a silly word. Try this: go to each person in your family and make a funny face. Try to get them to laugh. It will make them—and you—feel better.

69

Follow the Rules

"If you love me, you will do
the things I command."
John 14:15

Have you ever tried to play a game without rules?
One night at summer camp, the kids played a no-
rules basketball game. When the director, who is
John Luke and Sadie's other grandma (2-mama),
told everyone about the game, they thought it
would be fun. But soon everyone was running with
the ball and grabbing it from each other. Because
there were no rules, people were yelling and acting
crazy. Before you knew it, someone was hurt.

The kids learned this important lesson:
rules are there to make the game more fun!
Many times we think rules are mean or are just
something grown-ups decide to do to make kids
miserable, but that's not true. Almost everything
runs better when there are rules.

When you sit down to play any game, the first
thing you might ask is, "What are the rules?"
Knowing the rules makes the game more fun
to play! God's rules are called commandments.
God made rules or commandments because He

loves us and knows what we should do to live a good and happy life. This is true with your parents too. When God and your parents make a rule, listen carefully, because it is to help you, not hurt you. A life with no rules—just like a crazy basketball game with no rules—will hurt you.

Dear God, thank You for loving me enough to give me some rules to live by. Help me to always want to follow Your rules and to know that You love me. In Jesus' name, Amen.

DUCK Commander in ACTION

Find a deck of cards, and ask a friend or brother or sister to play with you. Pass out five cards to each player, and then pick up your cards. Tell them there are no rules to this game. It might get a little crazy, but you'll probably realize pretty quickly how important rules are.

God's Great Creations

Let them praise the Lord because they
were created by His command.
Psalm 148:5

When John Luke was a little boy, he loved his stuffed animals. At bedtime, he loved for Korie or Willie to make up stories about his stuffed animals coming to life. He had a *huge* collection of stuffed animals, and Willie might tell a story about his alligators swimming across the lake to have a picnic with his giraffes. It was fun! John Luke doesn't play with his stuffed animals anymore, but he still loves animals. Actually, he loves all of God's creation.

John Luke loves to be out in the woods fishing or just looking at everything God has made. It's good to go outside and look around because that's how we see God. It's hard to see God by watching TV or even by playing with your toys. Of course, God is there, too, but it's harder to see Him. Why? Because God is in His creation. When we look up at the sky and see the clouds floating by, we know God

made them. When we're really quiet at night, we can hear the birds coo or the crickets chirp, and we know God made them. God has blessed this earth with so many beautiful things; you don't have to look very far.

DUCK Commander in ACTION

Take a camera or a cell phone outside, and take pictures of ten things God made. Sit down and thank God for each of those things. He will be happy to hear from you!

Dear God, thank You for all the things You created. I want to always take care of Your creations and be thankful for them. In Jesus' name, Amen.

Celebrate God

Celebrate God all day, every
day. I mean, *revel* in him!
Philippians 4:4-5 MSG

One day, when Will was two years old, the family
was at the beach on the Fourth of July. They were
outside when the neighbors started celebrating
by shooting fireworks. Everyone discovered
quickly that Will did not like fireworks at all! He
ran into the house yelling, "Oh no!" Once he was
inside, he had fun watching the fireworks from the
window, but he didn't want to go back out where
the noise was. Popping fireworks on the Fourth
of July is a loud way to say thank you to the
men and women who fought for America. It's a
celebration of our country.

The Bible tells us to celebrate God.
Maybe we should pop firecrackers for
God? Willie's friend Charlie used to say to
live life "out loud and on purpose" for Jesus.
Firecrackers for God sure would be out loud!
Thankfully we don't have to be loud for God
to hear us. He hears our quietest whisper just

as easily as He hears our loudest scream. Anytime you are praying to Him or telling someone about Him or singing a song to Him, you are celebrating with Him—and He is listening. Any kind of celebration about God makes Him smile. He loves for His children to celebrate with Him. Every day with God is a party.

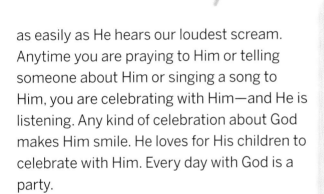
DUCK Commander in ACTION

It's time to party! Ask your mom to help you throw a party for Jesus. All you need is a colorful tablecloth and a cake. On top of the cake, use icing or candy to write "We love You, God" or "Go, God!" or anything else you want. Then celebrate God's goodness and love for you. Have fun!

Treat Others with Kindness

God has chosen you and made you his holy people. He loves you. So always do these things: Show mercy to others; be kind, humble, gentle, and patient.

Colossians 3:12

When Rebecca came to live with the Robertson family, she couldn't speak English very well. But that didn't stop her from wanting to play with the kids or the kids from wanting to play with her. She loved to play any kind of game and would try her best to understand the rules, but many times she would do the wrong thing. This taught her new brothers and sisters many things. They would have to speak more slowly and say the rules over and over to her. This taught them to be gentle and to say their words in a kind way. Because Rebecca didn't know how to play, the other kids had to be humble and not act like they were

better than she was. And because Rebecca kept making the same mistakes, they learned the gift of patience.

Learning to be kind, humble, gentle, and patient are great life lessons. In order for us to get along with our friends at school or our brothers and sisters, we need to be all of these things. It's not always easy being kind and patient, but it is the way God wants us to act, and it is the way we grow to be more like Him. Think about it: you want others to treat you with kindness and patience, so you need to treat them in the same way.

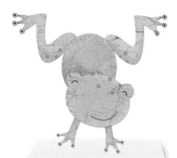

DUCK Commander in ACTION

One way to treat people with kindness is to give them a compliment. A compliment is saying something nice to someone. You might tell your mother that she has pretty hair or your brother that he is a hard worker. Go to five people and give them a compliment. You will change their day!

Dear God, thank You for Your kindness and patience with me. Help me to treat others as You treat me. In Jesus' name, Amen.

Go, Dad!

My children, listen to your father's teaching.
Pay attention so you will understand.
Proverbs 4:1

When John Luke was little he loved the movie *Bambi*. One of his favorite scenes was when Bambi stood beside his daddy. John Luke would stand up in bed and pretend he was the daddy deer. Now John Luke is proud to stand up beside his real daddy, Willie. He loves to hunt or go fishing with him. But mostly he is proud of Willie just because he is his daddy.

Our daddies are special to us. They take care of us and work hard for us. Sometimes it's not easy to be the dad of the family. Dads get up early and go to work every day so their families can have food to eat and a house to live in. Your dad might even coach a baseball team you play on or teach a Sunday school class. Dads do many things, but mostly they love us and want the best for us. That's why it's important to listen to our dads. The Bible tells us to "pay attention" to them. When your dad is talking to you, you should listen. That means putting down your video game or your book or whatever you are doing and really listening. This is how you show your dad that you think he's really special, and it honors God too.

DUCK Commander in ACTION

Even if it's not Father's Day, it's a good day to thank your dad for being a great dad. You don't need to give him a present; just tell him how much you love him and are thankful for him. You could make him a card, or just give him a huge hug and tell him how great he is. This will be a super great day for your dad. Have fun!

Dear God, thank You for my dad! I want to always honor him and listen to the words he says to me. Help me to be respectful to him always. In Jesus' name, Amen.

Going for the Goal

I keep trying to reach the goal
and get the prize. That prize
is mine because God called me
through Christ to the life above.

Philippians 3:14

Sadie loves to play basketball. She's a very good player and many times is the one who takes the ball all the way down the court. This is a very important—and hard!—job. The position is called point guard. Sadie has to know where all her teammates are, carefully bounce the ball, listen to her coach, and not listen to all the screaming fans watching the game. If she wants her team to win the game, she must do all these things—plus one more. She has to keep her eyes on the prize. Yes, in basketball, the only way to win a game is to put the basketball in the basket!

Have you ever set a goal? A goal is something you decide you are going to do, and then you do it—like deciding to eat more vegetables (seriously!) or learn how to play tennis (now *that's* fun). God wants us to set goals. He's a goal-setter too! He set a goal many years ago when He created the earth and then created *you*. The most important goal He wants all of us to set is to get to heaven. Once we set that goal, we have to focus like Sadie does when she plays basketball. We have to keep our eyes on that goal, look around for others who have the same goal, listen to our parents and teachers, and not listen to people who do not want the best for us. That's how you set your goal for God!

Lord, I want to keep my eyes on the goals You have for me—to get to heaven and to live for You. Help me to focus on the prize of living forever with You. In Jesus' name, Amen.

DUCK Commander in ACTION

Basketball is a fun game to play. If you have a basketball goal at your house, ask your mom or dad to go outside with you to play a game of B-I-B-L-E basketball. Every time you make a basket, you get to add a letter. See who can spell B-I-B-L-E first! If you don't have a basketball goal, just get a ball and a bucket, and aim for the bucket. Either way, you'll be reminded to keep your eyes on the goal!

Be a Leader

Remember your leaders. They
taught God's message to you.
Remember how they lived and
died and copy their faith.
Hebrews 13:7

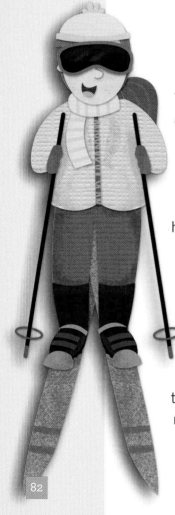

The Robertsons love to go snow skiing. One day while they were skiing, everyone decided to let Bella lead the way back to the vacation house. Bella was doing a great job—until she made a wrong turn. Bella's grandma (Bella calls her 2-mama) followed her. They went right over the side of a small mountain! No one was hurt, but they had to climb back up the mountain and walk a long way to the house.

Have you played the game Follow the Leader? It's a fun game where someone is the leader, and everyone has to do just what the leader does, or they are out of the game. Being a leader is a big job. That means other people are watching you and looking to you to guide them. Even though

Bella took a wrong turn, her family was proud of her for wanting to be a leader. God wants His people to be leaders in this world. God's people are great ones to lead others. That's because they are following God, who is the best leader! When we follow God, even if we take a wrong turn, He will be there to help us climb back up the hill of life.

Dear God, I want to be a leader in my school and at home. Help me to look to You for the right example and then to show others how to act. In Jesus' name, Amen.

Learn to Wait

I will look to the Lord for help. I
will wait for God to save me.
Micah 7:7

Bella and her cousins love to sell things in their neighborhood.
One day they made some lemonade and cake. They set up a table
with their treats and waited for the customers. But nobody came.
They waited and waited. Soon their grandpa showed up. He was so
excited to have a cool drink on a hot day. Then their aunt came by.
She was hungry, so she bought some of their cake. At the end of the
day, they had made ten dollars!

Bella and her cousins learned a lesson about being patient.
When no one came by their stand, some of her cousins wanted to
quit and go inside. But Bella wanted to wait. By waiting, good things
happened. Sometimes when we ask God to answer a prayer, we
want it to happen right now! But God always knows best, and He
will answer our prayers when it is the right
time. For most of us, being patient is
hard. We have to be willing to wait, and
waiting isn't easy.

What was the last thing you
had to wait for? Maybe you had
to wait for dinner to be cooked

or for your birthday to come so you could get a new toy. Waiting for dinner or a toy is hard, but it teaches us that patience is important and that good things will come if we just wait. The next time you pray, be willing to wait for God's answer. It will come right on time.

Dear God, it's hard to be patient! Help me learn to wait on You and to know that Your timing is perfect. In Jesus' name, Amen.

Practicing patience is hard! Try this: ask your mom if you can have a cookie or a piece of candy. Then put that cookie or piece of candy on a plate, and sit in front of it for five minutes. Set an alarm. After five minutes, think about how hard it was to wait to eat it. It is good practice for learning to wait for the good things in life.

Good Manners

Show respect for all people.
1 Peter 2:17

When Korie was a little girl, her mama used to tell her to use good table manners because she might grow up and eat at the White House with the President of the United States someday. For most of us, that will never happen, but Korie and Willie did grow up and eat at the White House! Now Korie's mom tells all the grandchildren the same thing.

Using good manners is a way of being respectful and considerate of others. It's about considering the feelings of other people and not just focusing on yourself. And it's not just good table manners; it's also saying "please" and "thank you" and "excuse me" wherever you go. Some other ways to show good manners are to hold the door open for others and to say hello to people when you see them.

When you show good manners to others, they are more likely to show good manners back to you. Back in the old days, children were taught to live by the

Golden Rule: Always do to others as you wish them to do to you. It's a good rule even today. If we all lived by this rule, the world would be a better place. Good manners could also be called *God manners* because God wants us to be considerate and respectful of everyone we meet. It's another way to spread God's love, and it makes everyone more pleasant to be around!

Dear God, I want to treat others with respect, and I know using good manners is a great way to do that. Help me to remember to use good manners in everything I do. In Jesus' name, Amen.

DUCK Commander in ACTION

Good manners aren't the same in every country. In some countries it's good manners to take off your shoes when you go inside, but in America that isn't necessary.

Learning all the good manners in America can seem confusing. Ask your mom and dad for help. You could start a manners poster to see how many manners you already know. This will be a great reminder for your whole family.

Give to Others

Each one should give, then, what he
has decided in his heart . . . God loves
the person who gives happily.
2 Corinthians 9:7

Every year, the Robertson family goes to the Dominican Republic
to help the people there. The Dominican Republic is an island in the
Atlantic Ocean, and many people in the Dominican don't have enough
food to eat or enough money to see a doctor when they are sick. The
Robertsons go with a group of people who can help in all these ways.
They deliver food and medicine to many families who need help.

One of the children there is named Maria. The Robertsons have
grown to love her very much. When they went to her house, they
noticed that her bed was broken, and she didn't have a pillow. Can
you imagine not having a pillow? So the Robertson family went to
the store and bought her a new bed and a pillow. When Maria came
home later and saw her new bed, she was so happy that she cried.
In fact, everyone cried because they were so happy to be able to
help little Maria! God's people have a job to do, and that job is to
help others whenever they can. When we help others, we show
them that they are loved. Everyone wants to feel loved. And the
amazing thing is that when you help someone, you will end up being
happy! That's how helping others works!

DUCK
Commander
in ACTION

There are many ways to help others. You don't have to go to another country either. People in our country need help too. Most cities have a food bank where they collect food to share with people who need it. Ask your parents if you can visit the food bank and help get food ready to give out. You could even fill a bag with food to take to your church so they can give it to someone who needs it.

Dear God, thank You for blessing my family. Help me to always look for others who need my help—and then to help them! In Jesus' name, Amen.

Sharing
Good News

How beautiful is the person who
comes to bring good news.
Romans 10:15

Have you ever gotten good news? Good news is
when you hear something that makes you excited
and happy. One day Sadie got some great news.
At Sadie's school, they celebrate Homecoming
with a football game, and they choose certain
girls to represent the school on the Homecoming
Court. Sadie was so honored to hear she had
been chosen to represent her school! That was
good news for sure, and Sadie wanted to share
it with the rest of the family. She started texting
everyone with her good news.

The best news *any* of us will ever hear is the
story of Jesus. It's the story of how Jesus came
to earth to teach people about
God. But then Jesus was put to
death by men who didn't believe
that He was the Son of God.

He was buried, but then something amazing happened—after three days, He rose from the grave to walk on the earth again for forty very important days. After those forty days, He went back up to heaven to sit on the right side of God. That's good news! Jesus came to earth just for us and is sitting by God still helping us. Now it's up to us to tell others this good news. Let's get started!

Dear God, help me to remember the good news of Jesus and to share it. I want to be ready to tell others about the sacrifice You made for me. In Jesus' name, Amen.

DUCK Commander in ACTION

Sharing good news is easy because it's fun to tell others when good things happen to us. We need to think about sharing God's message just like we think about sharing other good news. At our church family, we share the good news of Jesus with symbols. It looks like this:

These symbols tell the story of Jesus coming to earth, dying on the cross, being buried, going back to heaven, and coming to earth again. See if you can draw these symbols.

God's Earth

The earth and everything in it belong to the
Lord. The world and all its people belong to him.
He built it on the waters. He set it on the rivers.

Psalm 24:1-2

The Robertson family lives in Louisiana. The weather in Louisiana is usually warm, and it rains a lot. Because it rains a lot, there are lots of trees and flowers. Flowers and trees are just two of the many, many things God has created for us to enjoy.

Have you ever thought about *why* God gave us such beautiful things to look at? Our God is a God of many things. He is the God of love, peace, and hope, but He's also the God of beauty. Think about the mountains God created. In the winter they are covered with pure, white snow. Think about the ocean and how the water makes waves to wash over your feet. Think about the stars in the sky and how they twinkle and shine. No matter where you live, there is something beautiful about it because God wants us to have a beautiful place to live.

Sometimes we forget to be thankful for all the things God has created for us. When we see pretty flowers every day, we might get used to them and

walk right by without thinking about how beautiful they are and thanking God. Let's not forget about God's amazing creation. It's time to thank Him for a beautiful earth!

Dear God, thank You for all You have created. Help me not to forget what You have made and to appreciate all the beauty around me. In Jesus' name, Amen.

DUCK Commander in ACTION

If your mom has any coffee filters around the house, ask her if you can use one for a project (and a clothespin too!). Take your coffee filter and color it many different colors with either crayons or markers. Then pinch the coffee filter together in the middle, and clip it with the clothespin to make a flower. Write Psalm 24:1-2 on the clothespin to remind you that God created this beautiful earth.

Follow Jesus

Then a teacher of the law came
to Jesus and said, "Teacher, I will
follow you any place you go."
Matthew 8:19

If you have a little brother or sister, they probably like to follow you around. This happens a lot in the Robertson family. There are so many cousins, and the little cousins love to follow the older cousins. One day, the big cousins decided to run from Miss Kay's house to their aunt's house. But little River couldn't keep up with them, and he fell down and hurt his knee. Even though he hurt himself, the next time the big cousins wanted to go to their aunt's house, River *still* wanted to go.

When we follow someone we love, we don't mind if it's hard. River loves his older cousins and wants to follow them anywhere they go. The Bible tells us

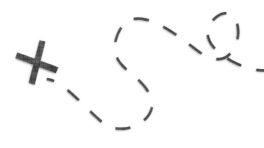

many stories about men and women following Jesus. Remember that in Bible times Jesus walked on this earth. But today, following Jesus means loving Him and obeying Him, telling others about Him, and learning more about Him. Following Jesus might mean going to another country or to a place in America that doesn't know about Jesus.

Here's the important thing to remember: following always means that you go with a leader. Jesus is our leader, and following is an action. If River wanted to follow his cousin, but he never left the house, he wouldn't be following them. To follow Jesus, we have to use our feet and go where He sends us.

DUCK Commander in ACTION

Take a piece of paper and pencil, and trace your foot. Then write the Scripture for today on that foot. This will remind you to go where Jesus sends you.

Dear God, I want to follow where You lead me. Help me to have feet that are ready to serve You. In Jesus' name, Amen.

God Knows
Our Feelings

If one of you is having troubles, he should pray.
If one of you is happy, he should sing praises.
James 5:13

Jesus had feelings just like you do. The Bible tells us that Jesus cried when His friend Lazarus died. We also know that He got angry when people were misusing the temple. And Jesus was happy when He healed sick men and women. It's good to know that Jesus understands us.

When Uncle Si was in the army, he was away from his family for a long time, and it made him sad. He knew that God understood how he felt, and he would pray to God for comfort. God knows there will be things that make us sad, just like there will be things that make us happy. We would like to be happy all the time! But it's okay to be sad sometimes. The Bible tells us to pray when we're sad. Praying through a hard time can make us stronger, and we learn to give our

hard times over to God. He will comfort us and help us get through them.

The Bible also tells us to sing when we're happy. That means we should let others know about our happiness. God loves you, and He wants to be there for your happy times *and* your sad times.

DUCK
Commander
in ACTION

Think of someone who you might want to cheer up, and make that person a happy card. You could draw a flower on it or maybe a balloon. You might want to write something like, *I'm thinking of you* or *God loves you.* You will make that person very happy today!

Dear God, thank You for loving me and understanding me. Help me to turn to You when I'm sad and to thank You when I'm happy. In Jesus' name, Amen.

Put Friends First

A friend loves you all the
time. A brother is always
there to help you.
Proverbs 17:17

Willie loves to collect things. He has baseball
cards of his favorite baseball players; he has old
records (large round discs that music used to be
played on); he collects Star Trek toys; he even
has a collection of Duck Dynasty things! If you
go to Willie's house, you will find his collections
in different places. Some of them are hanging on
a wall, and some are hidden away in a closet or a
drawer. If you ask him about them, he can tell you
every single thing about each of them. He loves
his collections, and they are very valuable to him.

Another thing Willie has collected over the
years is friends. He has friends who play baseball
and friends who are hunters. He has friends he
has known since he was
in kindergarten
and friends

he just met this year. As much as Willie loves his Star Trek collection, he loves his friends more. This is how we should all be. People are always more valuable and more important than our things. Willie knows that his baseball cards can't bring him food when he's sick or come to his house and cheer him up. Even though they are fun to have and look at, his baseball cards can't love him back.

Always remember to put people first. When we fight with our friends over some *thing*, we are not putting them first. We are saying that *thing* is more important than they are. A good friend will be with you all the time! Keep your friends number one!

Dear God, thank You for my friends. I know that You put them in my life especially for me. Help me never to put my things before my friends. In His name, Amen.

God Is Always with Us

You are all around me—in front and in
back. You have put your hand on me.
Psalm 139:5

The Robertsons love to go on vacation together. Sometimes they will have six houses at the beach filled with family members! Or they go to Disney World or Silver Dollar City. All the Robertson men play golf on their vacation and the women go shopping or to the waterpark. They try not to think about work and just enjoy being together. Maybe your family loves to go on vacation too. Most people do. A vacation doesn't have to be far from home or at a fancy place. It's just a time when families can get away from work and have fun together.

Do you think God ever takes a vacation? Do you think He plays golf or rides a roller coaster? That's funny to think about, isn't it? God could do those things, but He doesn't because He's always busy watching over us. Have you ever gone into your parents' room at night and before you could say anything, your mom or dad woke up? They could feel that you were there and needed them. God is like that all the time. The Bible tells us He is all around us, in front of us and behind us, and He never sleeps. That should make us feel great! We can always depend on God to be our friend, our helper, our provider, our peacemaker. He is always there!

DUCK Commander in ACTION

Vacations give us time away from our other work, like school or chores around our house. Just like God never takes time off from us, we should never take time off from God. In fact, we should plan time *with* God. Read or have someone read Psalm 139 to you, and talk about or write down all the ways and times God is with you.

Dear God, thank You for always being with me. I want to be with You all the time too. In Jesus' name, Amen.

You Are God's Treasure

For you are a people holy to
the LORD your God. Out of all
the peoples on the face of the
earth, the LORD has chosen you
to be his treasured possession.

Deuteronomy 14:2 NIV

Miss Kay has a special recipe for biscuits. She says they have a secret ingredient to make them extra yummy. That special ingredient is sour cream. If you were to eat a big spoonful of sour cream, you might spit it out. It's sour! But when it's hidden in a certain recipe, it makes that cake or pie or biscuit *AMAZING!* Sour cream is kind of a hidden treasure.

Did you know that you are God's treasure? You aren't really hidden, but you are definitely a treasure. A treasure is anything that has special value or meaning to someone. If you're a girl, a necklace your grandmother gave you might be your best treasure. If you're a boy, an old watch handed down from your dad might be a treasure. The important thing about treasures is that they bring you joy and are very valuable to you.

When God says YOU are His treasure, He means YOU bring Him joy and are very valuable *to Him*. Treasures are also treated in a special way. If you have a special necklace or watch, you might keep it in a secret or safe place and take good care of it. That's what God does with YOU. He hides you in His heart, and He takes really good care of YOU!

DUCK Commander in ACTION

It's time for a treasure hunt! On a piece of paper, draw a heart, color it red, and write the word *ME* in the middle of the heart. Cut out the heart, and hide it in a special place—but someplace where you will see it every day. When you see it each day, remind yourself that YOU are special.

Dear God, thank You for making ME Your treasure. Thank You for hiding me in Your heart and for taking good care of me. In Jesus' name, Amen.

The Word
Lights the Way

*Your word is like a lamp for my
feet and a light for my way.*

Psalm 119:105

Have you ever walked through your garage in the dark? It's pretty scary, isn't it? Your garage probably has a car, a trash can, and maybe a bicycle in it. Those things aren't scary, are they? But when you can't see something, it becomes scary. Korie lives next door to her mom, so they spend a lot of time walking back and forth. They always have to pass through the garage to get to the back door. If Korie didn't have some kind of light, she might trip over a bicycle or hit her knee on a trash can. So her daddy put up a big light in their driveway so nobody can get hurt coming to see them.

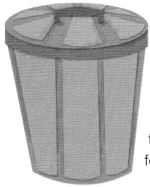

Light is very important to us. A long time ago, people had to depend on fire to give them light at night. We have electricity now, but when the power goes out, we remember pretty quickly how important light is. The writer of Psalm 119 compared God's Word to a light. He knew this would be a good way for people to understand that the Bible is very important. We can't live without light, and the Bible is even more important than light! Just like a light leads us in the right direction, so does God's Word. Use your Bible today to shine a light on your path.

Dear God, thank You for giving us Your Word. Help me to understand the Bible and to want to know more about You. In Jesus' name, Amen.

DUCK Commander in ACTION

Get a flashlight, and find a room in your house that has no windows. Take your Bible with you. Shut the door and turn off the light. Sit for a few minutes in the dark to see if your eyes adjust to the dark. After a few minutes, turn on your flashlight and look up the Bible verse for the day. Use your flashlight to read the verse and say your prayers.

God Works for Us

We know that in everything
God works for the good
of those who love him.

Romans 8:28

The Robertsons own a company called Duck Commander. Duck Commander builds duck calls, and all the family works there. Because they love the company and their family, they would never do anything to hurt the family business. God loves each of us just like the Robertsons love their Duck Commander company. Because He loves us, He wants what is best for us. Does that mean He will give us everything we want? No! God loves us enough *not* to give us everything we want. But He will give us everything we need. In fact, the Bible tells us that God works for us! Isn't that cool? Usually bosses (like Willie) have people who work for them, but our God, who is our boss, works for us! Think about it like this: God is the boss of the whole world, and He doesn't want anything bad to happen to His people, so He's always working to help them. Does that mean nothing bad will ever happen? No. But it means when bad things do happen, God is hard at work to help us get through them. Your parents are like this too. They are the boss of you, but because they love you, they work to make your life safe, comfortable, and fun.

DUCK Commander in ACTION

Being the boss is a hard and important job. It means everyone looks to you to tell them what to do. Ask your mom if you can switch with her for a few hours. You be the mom, and let her be the kid. This way you will understand what your mom has to do to be the "boss" of your family. It might be harder than you think!

Dear God, thank You for always working *for* me. Help me to understand the difference between what I want and what I need. In Jesus' name, Amen.

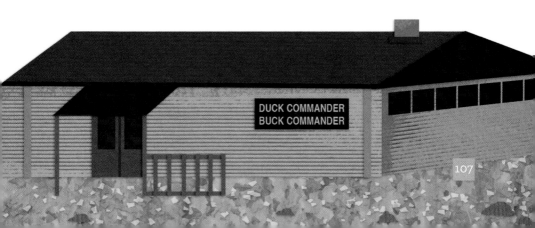

DUCK COMMANDER
BUCK COMMANDER

God Is Invisible But Always There

There are things about God that people cannot see—his eternal power and all the things that make him God. But since the beginning of the world those things have been easy to understand. They are made clear by what God has made.

Romans 1:20

Phil has several boats. On most days, you can find him fishing somewhere. In order for his boat to move down the water, it needs a motor. A motor has blades on it that move very fast. When you're in the boat, you can't see the blades. You know they are there because the boat is moving, but they're under the water so you can't see them.

That's how our mighty God is. He is all-powerful, and we can't know everything about how He is working. We can see all that He does though, so we know He is there. Can you think of some other things you can't see but you know are there and working? What about the wind? Or germs? Or electricity?

Believing in things we can't see is part of life. Even though we can't see God, we see His creation and know He exists. We feel the warmth of the sun He created and watch the flowers He planted bloom. When there isn't lightning, it's fun to run outside in the rain and feel the water God provides for the earth. Yes, there are things we will never know about God, but we *can* know He exists!

Dear God, thank You for showing me that You are real! I want to be more thankful for all the things You've given me as a reminder of Your great love. In Jesus' name, Amen.

Love Your Neighbor

"And the second command is like the first: 'Love your neighbor as you love yourself.'"

Matthew 22:39

One day Phil went out to check his fishing nets. As he got closer to the nets, he saw some teenage boys pulling in his nets and getting his fish. Phil had a decision to make: Was he going to get mad? Or was he going to teach them an important lesson? Phil chose to teach an important lesson. Instead of yelling at the boys, he told them they could get as many fish as they needed. The boys looked at him like he was crazy! How could he be so nice when they were stealing his fish? Phil had come to understand that God blesses those who are kind to others, even if they are doing the wrong thing.

You see, it's not the other person's behavior that makes a difference—it's *our* behavior. How do you react when someone else is doing the wrong thing? Do you get mad or cry or yell at them? The Bible tells us to love our neighbor as ourselves. Sometimes we know our neighbor, and sometimes we don't. A neighbor is anyone who lives around us. Even if we don't know someone, the best way to treat that person is with love and kindness. Because Phil showed kindness toward these teenage boys, they were able to see God in him. And they never stole his fish again.

Dear God, thank You for loving me. I want to love my neighbors like You love me. Help me to put others first and to show them that I love them too. In His name, Amen.

DUCK Commander in ACTION

Showing kindness or love to our neighbors can be done in many ways. You might want to bake cookies and take them next door, or you might want to pick up trash or leaves in your neighbor's yard. Whatever you do, remember that you are showing your neighbor that God's love lives in you.

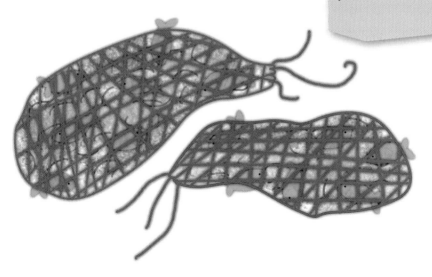

God Provides

Who gives food to the birds when their young
cry out to God? And who gives them food
when they wander about without any?

Job 38:41

When Phil and Miss Kay were first married, they didn't have much money. Phil was just starting his duck call business, and they weren't selling very many. Miss Kay was in charge of paying the bills. One month, when it came time to pay the bills, she told Phil they didn't have enough money. Phil did everything he could to make more money, but it wasn't going to be enough. Phil told Miss Kay to go check the mailbox. "Maybe someone will pay their bill," he told Miss Kay. But Miss Kay knew no one owed them anything. Phil went to the mailbox anyway. He pulled out an envelope from Japan. In the envelope was an order for duck calls and a check for eight hundred dollars! It was the exact amount of money they needed to pay their bills.

Phil believes that God provided for them that day and still provides for them. It wasn't more than they needed. It was *exactly* what they needed. When we trust God to handle our business, He will do it. A man named Job in the Bible asked the question, "Who gives the birds the food they need?" Do *you* know the answer to that question? If you said "God," then you are right. God takes care of the animals, and He will take care of you too. You just have to ask and then count on Him!

Dear God, thank You for always providing for me and for the other creatures on the earth. You are an awesome God. You know what I need before I even tell You! In Jesus' name, Amen.

DUCK Commander in ACTION

As a kid, you depend on your mom and dad to provide things like food, clothes, and a house. Your parents are God's way of helping you until you are old enough to do it yourself. The animals depend on God to provide those things.

Go on a nature hike, and take a picture of everything you see that can be used for food for some of God's creatures. You might take a picture of a flower or a worm or a seed. Have fun!

Listen Up!

*"Whoever belongs to God
hears what God says."*

John 8:47 NIV

All the Robertson boys played baseball when they were growing up, and now the grandkids play. Will is a teenager now, but when he was little, he played tee-ball. Have you ever played tee-ball? One day Will hit the ball and ran to first base. But he didn't stop there! He kept running all the way to the outfield. He wasn't the only one on the team not doing the right thing. The catcher was sitting on the ground playing in the dirt. The players in the outfield were fighting over a ball. It seemed like there was no coach at all!

But the team did have a coach, and he was trying to get their attention. He would yell, "Run, run, run!" but the kids weren't listening. Sometimes the coach would take a player by his shoulders and put him where he needed to be. That coach was working really hard; the kids just weren't listening. Sometimes we do the same thing to God, don't we? He tries to tell us what we should do, but we don't listen to Him. He

tells us through the Bible and through our parents and our Bible teachers. God *always* has the right thing to say to us, the words that will help us to succeed and be safe. He loves us and wants us to have a good life. Just like a good coach does, God will lead you in the right direction if you just listen to Him.

> **Thank You, God, for giving me ears to hear. Be with me each day, and help me listen to Your plan for my life. In Jesus' name, Amen.**

Did you know that listening is a choice? There are times when our ears might be able to hear, but we choose *not* to actually listen. When your brother or sister is talking too much, you might choose not to listen. But we should all choose to listen to God. You can even practice listening. Try this: have your friends sit in a circle. Someone starts the game by whispering one sentence into the ear of the next person. That person then whispers what he heard to the next person. Once the last person has heard the sentence, he or she will say it out loud. It will be fun to see how well everyone listened.

God Will Help

But if any of you needs wisdom, you
should ask God for it. God is generous.
He enjoys giving to all people . . . But
when you ask God, you must believe.

James 1:5-6

Korie and Willie always wanted to adopt a child, but they didn't know when or how. They prayed that God would answers their prayers for another baby when *He* was ready, not when they were ready. One day they got a call from a children's home in Louisiana about a baby boy who needed a good family. The children's home sent them a picture of Will, and they knew he was their baby. So they said, "Yes!"

They finished filling out all the adoption papers and went to pick up baby Will. From the minute they saw him, they knew God had answered their prayers with this son. They named him Will Alexander after Willie and Phil, whose middle name is Alexander.

God doesn't answer just one prayer and stop though. Over the years, Korie and Willie have asked God for wisdom as parents. God has always been there for them and will never leave them. He is here to help them and to help **YOU**! But we have to remember that God answers our prayers according to what is *really* best for us, not what we *think* is best for us. And we can trust Him to do just the right thing at just the right time.

Dear God, thank You for letting me talk to you. When I am sad or happy, I know You are there for me. I want to be closer to You! In Jesus' name, Amen.

DUCK Commander in ACTION

Have you ever tried to get your mom's attention when you were in the backyard and she was in the house? It's pretty hard to do, isn't it? She's too far away! Even though God can always hear you, He wants you to get closer to Him so He can *really* hear you, and so you can be better friends. You get closer to God by reading the Bible, going to church, and praying. Look up 1 Thessalonians 5:17 to find out how often we should pray.

Obey Your Parents

Children, obey your parents in
all things. This pleases the Lord.
Colossians 3:20

John Luke is always ready for an adventure. When he was six years old, he and Willie were exploring the land around their house and found a bat. The bat was sick, so they decided to nurse it back to good health. This can be dangerous, so Willie and Korie warned John Luke to never touch the bat. John Luke found a pair of rubber gloves and decided maybe he could pick up the bat if he had the gloves on. But when he picked up the bat, it bit him on his little finger! Korie had to take John Luke to the hospital, where he had to get lots of shots.

The Bible tells us that obeying our parents will please the Lord. Obeying our parents also keeps us safe. If John Luke had obeyed Korie and Willie, he wouldn't have had to get all those shots. Our parents want the best for us, so when they ask us to do something, we need to remember that

it's for our own good. Even doing things like cleaning your room is for your own good. One day you will be on your own and will need to know how to keep it clean. So from small things, like brushing your teeth, to big things, like, "Don't touch that bat!" obeying your parents is a good thing to do.

Dear God, thank You for my parents. I love them and want to obey them. Sometimes I make the wrong choices. Help me to listen and obey. In His name, Amen.

DUCK Commander in ACTION

Have you ever played a game called Mother, May I? It was probably invented by a mom who was teaching her children to obey. Here's how you play: One person has to be the mom. She then asks her children to take a certain number of steps toward her. But before they can move, they have to say, "Mother, May I?" If they move and forget to say those words, they have to go back to the beginning. The one who reaches the mom first wins. Find some friends and play this fun game.

Names for God

I will announce the name of the Lord.
Praise God because he is great!
Deuteronomy 32:3

What names do you have for each of your grandmas? Some grandmas are called Mimi. Some are called Nana. But when John Luke was little, he insisted on calling his grandma *and* his mama the same thing: Mama. This was very confusing. They never knew who he was calling! This grandma is not Miss Kay; it is Korie's mom. Korie and her mom tried many different grandma names, but none of them seemed to work. One day, after Sadie was born, John Luke looked up at his grandma and called her "2-Mama." And that was it. That is her grandma name, and now all the grandkids and their friends call her 2-Mama.

Names are important, aren't they? Everything and everyone has a name. We get used to what something is named. If we were to call it by another name, it would be silly. Think about using the word *chair* for a table. That would be crazy! We usually have one name for one person or thing, but God has *many* names. His names

describe Him. The names are in the Hebrew language, but we can translate them to English. Here are some of the names for God: *Adonai*, which means Lord Master; *Elohim*, which means My Creator; *El Shaddai*, which means God Almighty. Learning the different names for God helps us to know Him better.

Dear God, I love to learn more about You. Your name is all-powerful and mighty, and I always want to honor that. In His name, Amen.

Always Tell the Truth

You must not say evil things. You must not lie.
Psalm 34:13

Willie has an older brother named Alan. Alan used to wake Willie up late at night and tell him it was time for school. Willie would get up and get dressed before Alan would tell him he was joking with him. Of course, this made Willie very mad, and he would run after Alan to fight him.

Alan was just teasing Willie. You may have done something like this to one of your brothers or sisters, but Alan told Willie a lie. It wasn't really time for school, and Willie didn't need to get up. A lie is something that is not true and usually leads to more trouble. Sometimes people lie to try to stay out of trouble or to get attention from their friends.

Telling the truth is the opposite of telling a lie. When others can depend on you to tell them truth, you will become good

friends. They will learn to trust you. Trust is what makes any relationship better. Lying can become a bad habit, so it's a great idea *never* to lie. That way you don't have to worry about it.

DUCK Commander in ACTION

There are some great books about telling the truth. Get one of these great books and have fun reading and learning. *The Berenstain Bears and the Truth* or *Little Critters It's True* are good ones.

Dear God, help me to always tell the truth. I want others to be able to trust me. I want my words to make You proud. In Jesus' name, Amen.

Be Grace-Filled

Grace, mercy, and peace will be with us from God
the Father and from his Son, Jesus Christ. And
may we have these blessings in truth and love.
2 John v. 3

Do you know what *grace* is? You might know a little girl named Grace, or maybe that's what you call prayer before a meal at your house, or maybe you heard the word used at church. You may have heard about grace at church because it is what we say God has done for us. He offers us *grace*.

So what is grace? Grace is when you *don't* get what you deserve. What does that mean? Here's an example. One time Willie and Jase were fighting (yes, they did that a lot as kids!). This time Jase started it by pushing Willie out of his chair. Willie was mad and got up to fight him, but Miss Kay came in the room. Both of the boys deserved to get in trouble, but Miss Kay was in a good mood and neither boy got in trouble. She gave them grace.

God has given us great big grace! We are all sinners. We deserve to be punished for our sins. But that isn't what God does! Instead, God forgives us and shows us grace and gives us blessings because He loves us. That is grace. We don't get what we deserve (punishment), and we do get what we don't deserve (forgiveness and blessings).

We can offer other people grace by not saying something mean back to them when they are mean to us. We can give grace when we forgive a friend who has done something wrong to us. Grace is also when you choose to ignore a comment your brother or sister says to you. These are some ways we don't give other people what they deserve. That is how to be grace-filled.

Dear God, please fill me up with grace. Help me to forgive others like You have forgiven me and to treat everyone I meet with Your grace. In Jesus' name, Amen.

DUCK Commander in ACTION

Look up John 1:16, and fill in the blanks: "The Word was full of

_____

and _____. From him we all received more and more _____."

Handling Disappointments

Give all your worries to him,
because he cares for you.
1 Peter 5:7

We all get disappointed, don't we? Sadie really wanted to be a cheerleader, so when she didn't make the team, she was disappointed. Being disappointed is part of life. We will all be disappointed at some point in our lives. What we don't have to do is *stay* disappointed. Sadie allowed herself to be disappointed for a short time, and then she got on with life. She was still a basketball player, a tennis player, a student, and a great kid. She just wasn't a cheerleader. Sadie learned a valuable lesson by not making the team—she learned how to handle disappointment.

Even God gets disappointed. In the Bible, we read about good men disappointing God. One of them was Moses. Moses struck a rock instead of speaking to it, as God commanded him to do. God was surely sad for a little while when He realized that Moses had disobeyed Him. But God had other work to do, so He didn't stay sad for long. When something disappoints you, learn to get over it quickly. Look for ways to use your talents for good. Turn your attention to something else.

Dear God, I get disappointed sometimes. Help me to handle my disappointment in the best way— to always turn to You and let You guide me to a better place. In Jesus' name, Amen.

Passing the Test

When a person is tempted and still
continues strong, he should be happy.
James 1:12

Why do you take tests in school? If you answered, "To see how well we know the information the teacher taught us," you are right! You've passed this little test. When you pass a test in school, it makes you feel good. Most of the time, you do well on a test because you've studied and prepared for it. Most of the Robertson grandkids are learning a musical instrument. They all work hard at their different instruments and practice on most days. A few times a year, they have a recital. It's always easy to tell which kids at the recital have been practicing. They are the kids who do the best. The recital is a type of test.

Life is full of tests too. As you get older, you will see many life tests. For example, one test that life might give you is if someone

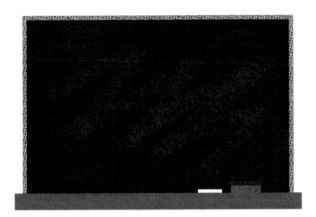

you know tries to get you to do something you shouldn't do. Or maybe you get sick right before a big day at school or an activity you were looking forward to. Life's tests can be very challenging and sometimes a surprise. We don't get to practice for them like we practice for our piano recital. What we do get is a God who will help us to stay strong and will give us what we need to pass life's tests.

DUCK Commander in ACTION

Memorize Proverbs 3:6 with these hand signals: "Remember (point to your head) the Lord (point to the sky) in everything (open your arms wide open) you do. And He (point to sky) will give you success (bring your elbows down onto your waist for a *yes!* motion)."

Dear God, thank You for the tests in my life. They help me learn to depend on You. In Jesus' name, Amen.

Be Careful of Pride

A man's pride will ruin him. But a person
who is humble will be honored.
Proverbs 29:23

What letter is in the middle of the word *pride*? The letter *I* is right in the middle! That might be because pride is full of I, I, I, with no room for anyone else. Yes, pride is thinking that you are more important than anyone else around you. This is not a good way to be and actually goes against everything good about God. Phil Robertson has said many times that if the TV show causes them to have trouble as a family, they will stop being on TV. They will not let pride in the show come before their family.

Pride was what got Eve in trouble in the Bible. She thought she deserved all that Satan promised her, so she gave in to what he told her to do. Pride starts in the heart when we do things for the wrong reason. You might help your teacher clean her room, which is a good thing. But if you do it so

she'll give you a better grade, then it's for the wrong reason. Be careful and guard your heart against prideful thinking. Instead, be humble, which is always about putting the feelings of others first.

It's okay to be proud of things like your school or your family, but having pride about your own accomplishments is a wrong choice. When you have a talent like singing or sports, God gave you that talent to begin with. Don't be prideful; be grateful. List the things you are capable of doing, and then thank God for blessing you with those abilities.

Dear God, thank You for my talents and accomplishments. I want to use them to show others about _You_, not me! In Jesus' name, Amen.

Overcoming Mistakes

We all make many mistakes. If there
were a person who never said anything
wrong, he would be perfect.

James 3:2

Miss Kay is a great cook! Everyone loves to eat at her house. But one day she was making fried shrimp, and she put too much batter on the shrimp. Phil told her he couldn't even see the shrimp! From that day on, Phil has been the shrimp-cooker in the family.

We all make mistakes. Some of the mistakes we make are simple, like messing up the shrimp. But other mistakes can hurt people we love. A mistake is different than a sin. A sin is messing up against God by breaking one of His rules, but a mistake is just making a bad decision or a poor choice. One time, a friend of the Robertsons put the wrong kind of gas in the four-wheeler. That wasn't a sin. It was a mistake, and it cost a lot of money to fix it.

There's an easy fix to most mistakes. All you have to do is confess what you did and ask the person to forgive you. And one more thing: learn from that mistake and don't do it again! Usually that's all it takes to turn a *mess* into a *message*.

Dear God, I don't want to make mistakes. But when I do, help me to learn from them, to ask for forgiveness, and to move on quickly. In Jesus' name, Amen.

DUCK
Commander
in ACTION

Ask your mom if you can start a mistake jar. Find a glass jar and write the words *Mistake Jar* on the outside. Whoever makes a mistake has to add some money to the jar. Your mom can help you decide how much money to put in according to the mistake. When you have enough money, the whole family can go get a treat. That will show everyone that messes can end up as good messages!

Protect Yourself

But the Lord is faithful. He will give you
strength and protect you from the Evil One.

2 Thessalonians 3:3

Korie loves to snow ski. She has skied every year since she was five years old. On her first ski trip, she went with her grandpa and grandma, and no one warned them about the sun in the high mountains. The sun was very bright, and Korie didn't wear any sunscreen. Her cheeks got so burned they were one big blister! Grandpa, Grandma, and Korie all learned the value of protection.

There are other ways we protect ourselves. Can you think of some of them? We wear seatbelts in our cars and helmets when we ride bikes. We wear life jackets when we swim in the lake and sunscreen when we go to the beach. Yes, all of these are ways to protect us from something bad happening to us, like Korie's sunburn. But our real protection, our greatest protection, comes from God, our heavenly Father. The verse for today tells us that God is

faithful in His protection against the evil one. Satan is the evil one, and you don't have to apply any lotion or cream to protect yourself against him; you just have to put on God.

We all know ways to be safe. Being safe against Satan means to put on God. Read Ephesians 6:10–17, and write down the armor God provides for your protection. It will be more powerful than a huge bottle of sunscreen!

Dear God, thank You for Your armor of protection! Help me when I face trials and temptations by guarding me against the evil one. In Jesus' name, Amen.

Remember to Be Respectful

Show respect for all people. Love the
brothers and sisters of God's family.
Respect God. Honor the king.

1 Peter 2:17

One of Willie's favorite Bible school teachers is a lady named Miss Willa. He loves Miss Willa and looks for her at church to give her a hug and a smile. He shows respect to Miss Willa in this way for many reasons: he loves her, she was his teacher when he was younger, she is older than he is, and she is a sister in God's family. But those aren't the only reasons!

A long time ago, God instructed His people to respect all people. Do you know what *respect* means? It means to treat others

with kindness and love. The Bible verse above says to respect "all people." That includes your teachers, the lady driving the car next to you, the man who serves you at a restaurant, and everyone else you see in a day. Respect means honoring those in authority by listening to them and doing what is asked of you. Notice that God doesn't ask us to be respectful only if the person deserves it. God asks us to be respectful out of love for *Him*. Our love for God is why we respect others. It is God's love that will shine through when we show others that we respect them.

Dear God, help me to respect those in authority over me. I know this is part of Your plan for my life. In Jesus' name, Amen.

Be a Good Example

You are young, but do not let anyone treat you as if you were not important. Be an example to show the believers how they should live. Show them with your words, with the way you live, with your love, with your faith, and with your pure life.

1 Timothy 4:12

When Phil started making duck calls, he didn't think anyone else could make them as good as he could. But when so many people wanted them, he had to train his son Jase to make them too. He was surprised to discover that Jase could do it just as good as he could! Soon the company grew even bigger, and Phil and Jase had to teach more people how to build a duck call. One day Phil came in the duck call room where six people were building duck calls and said, "Well, I guess it's not that hard to build a duck call after all." The truth is that it isn't difficult if you have a good example to follow.

Jase and Phil were both good examples to follow. They love to build duck calls and take pride in doing a good job. This makes it easy for someone else to follow them. What kind of example are you? Do you take pride in how you live? Do you make it easy for someone to follow you and do the right thing? The Bible tells us to be a good example to others by the words we use, the actions we take, and the love we show. God needs people like Phil, Jase, and *you* to stand up for Jesus.

Dear God, let me be a good example to everyone around me. I want to follow in Jesus' footsteps. In Jesus' name, Amen.

DUCK Commander in ACTION

Being a good example means you let others see you doing good. This will encourage them to do good too. Smiling is a good way to bring joy to others. And smiles are contagious. *Contagious* means others will catch on—if you do it, then they'll do it too. Try smiling at everyone you meet today. Count how many people smile back at you.

Don't Give Up

We say they are happy because they were
able to do this. You have heard about
Job's patience. You know that after all his
trouble, the Lord helped him. This shows
that the Lord is full of mercy and is kind.

James 5:11

Sometimes it seems like we can't do anything right. When Phil was trying to build the world's best duck call, he took his design idea to a friend at church who was already building duck calls. The man looked at Phil's idea and said it would never work. He told Phil it was too small. Phil was not discouraged, and he didn't change his mind. He knew he had the right size. He went back to his shop and kept working on his duck call. Today he has sold millions of duck calls. He never gave up, and it paid off. When things are not going our way, it's easy to want to give up. We get discouraged. We have to remember that it's the challenges in life that make us better and help us grow up. When that man told Phil his duck call was too small, Phil could have said, "Okay, I'm done." But he didn't. He just had to work harder. You might get discouraged at times, but hang in there! If what you are doing is a good thing, God will bless you. It just might take a little longer.

Dear God, thank You for being patient with me and for never giving up. Help me not to get discouraged and to stay strong when things are hard. In Jesus' name, Amen.

DUCK Commander in ACTION

Doing hard things will make us stronger. We know that exercise makes our bodies stronger. Today, do ten push-ups, ten jumping jacks, and ten sit-ups. By the time you get to the last one, it might be hard. But don't give up! This will remind you to keep trying in everything you do in life.

Love Your Enemies

"I tell you, love your enemies.
Pray for those who hurt you.
If you do this, you will be true
sons of your Father in heaven."
Matthew 5:44-45

It's easy to love those people who love you back, isn't it? But what about the people who don't love you? The people who are actually mean to you. Did you know the Bible tells us to love them too? It does. One day Phil was supposed to be on TV with some musicians. But the musicians decided they didn't want to be on the same show as Phil, so they didn't appear. A reporter asked Phil what he thought about the musicians. He said, "I love them anyway."

Wow! That's a hard thing to do, isn't it? To love someone who doesn't love you back. But it's the right thing to do. In fact, the Bible tells us to love them and to pray for them. There will be times when you don't want to love someone. It might a kid in your class who has been mean to you, or it might be your brother who keeps touching your things. People can just be annoying sometimes! But those are the times when you need to pray for them and learn to love them anyway.

Dear God, help me to be more patient with others. Help me to forgive when I need to and to love everyone. In Jesus' name, Amen.

DUCK Commander in ACTION

One way to forgive others is to remember that we have problems too. Here's a way to help you remember: Take your pointer finger and point it at another person or out in the air. You will notice that one finger points out, but all the others point back to you. We all do things that are annoying, aggravating, and sometimes unkind. It will make it easier to love your enemies when you realize you make mistakes too.

Sharing

Tell the rich people to do good and to be rich in doing good deeds. Tell them to be happy to give and ready to share.

1 Timothy 6:18

When Phil and Miss Kay were first married, they didn't have much money. In fact, they didn't even have enough money to buy the oil they needed to fry fish. So they came up with a plan. They would share oil with Phil's brother Tommy and his wife, Nancy. The oil was kept in a big cast-iron pot, and every week they would carry the pot from house to house. It took a lot of work to share, but it was worth it. Both families got to enjoy a fish fry for half the money!

Sharing with others is a gift we give someone else. When you are willing to let a friend play with your toys or give

your little sister a piece of your candy, you are saying that you love that person enough to let her have something of yours. While sharing is an act of kindness, it doesn't mean you have to give up what you have immediately or every time you're asked. You should try your best to work it out. If someone wants to play with the toy you are playing with, you can politely say, "Sure, in just a few minutes, when I am done." And remember that this works both ways. You have to be patient with others when you want something they have.

Dear God, thank You for all the things You have given me. Help me to share what I have with others. Help me to be patient when I want others to share with me. In Jesus' name, Amen.

DUCK Commander in ACTION

It's easy to think about sharing when you're not asked to share, but it's hard to do when someone wants something that is yours. By using each letter in the word *SHARE*, think of an object that you might share with a friend or family member. *S* could be shoes or a soaker gun. *H* could be helicopter. Now you think of words that start with *A*, *R*, and *E*. Practice sharing these things with an imaginary friend.

Who Do You Belong To?

"Once you had no identity as a people; now you are God's people. Once you received no mercy; now you have received God's mercy."

1 Peter 2:10 NLT

If you watch *Duck Dynasty* you know that Uncle Si was in the army. When someone is in the army, he or she is given a necklace to wear called a dog tag. That dog tag has information about the soldier on it. It has his or her name, social security number, branch of service (Army, Navy, or Marine), and religion. A dog tag is very important to a soldier. If he is hurt and can't talk, a dog tag will help get him home. A dog tag tells a soldier's identity. An *identity* is who someone is and where they belong. Everyone's identity is different because every person is different. There's one part of Uncle Si's identity that is just like many other people: Uncle Si loves God and believes in God, so he is a child of God—one of God's children.

Uncle Si lives in Louisiana, wears glasses, drinks iced tea, drives a truck, makes duck calls, hunts, and fishes, but the most important thing he does is live for God! That's where his true identity is found. When you love God, you are His child, and you get to put that on your dog tag!

Dear God, thank You for choosing *me* to be Your child and that my identity is in You. Help me to never be afraid to tell others that I belong to You. In His name, Amen.

DUCK Commander in ACTION

You can easily make your own dog tag with some heavy cardstock paper. Cut it into a rectangle shape with rounded corners. If you want to make it look silver, cover it in aluminum foil. With a hole punch, punch a hole in the top. Attach a string to hang it around your neck. Use a permanent marker to write your name, and then write *Child of God* under your name.

Choose Wisely

"I am allowed to do all things." But all things are not good for me to do.
1 Corinthians 6:12

Rebecca is Korie and Willie's foster daughter. A foster child is someone who comes to live with a family, but wasn't born into the family. Rebecca was born in Taiwan. She has a family in Taiwan who loves her very much, but she wanted to go to school in America. She came to America when she was sixteen. She finished college and is now living and working in Louisiana with her American family, the Robertsons.

When she first came to America, she loved everything about it. It was very different from Taiwan. One thing she loved was the food. She loved it so much that she couldn't stop eating it! She gained thirty pounds the first year she was in America because she loved ice cream and candy so much. Soon Rebecca learned that just because something tasted good and she was allowed to eat it, that didn't mean it was good for her. The Bible talks about this very thing. There are many things that seem good to us and we are allowed to do them, but they are *not* good for us. That is why God gave us our brains, so we can choose wisely the things that are good or bad for us. Rebecca still loves American food, but she's learned to use her brain and to watch what she eats. She makes wise choices.

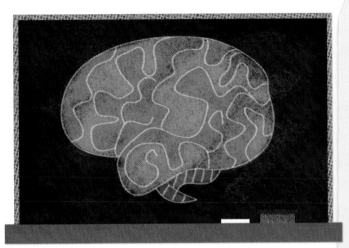

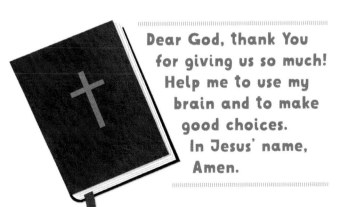

Dear God, thank You for giving us so much! Help me to use my brain and to make good choices. In Jesus' name, Amen.

Aren't we blessed to have our brains? Our brains are the computer system for our whole body. When you move your arm or leg, it's your brain that tells it to move. Our brains can get trained to do certain things. Clasp your hands together with your fingers locked together. Now unlock your fingers and lock them back, but this time move them over to lock in a different place. That feels strange, doesn't it? When we decide to change something, it might seem strange at first, but soon you will get used to it. If you need to change something, today's a good day to start.

Don't Worry—
Trust God

"So don't worry, because I
am with you. Don't be afraid,
because I am your God. I will
make you strong and will help
you. I will support you with my
right hand that saves you."

Isaiah 41:10

Do you know what it means to worry? Worry is what we do when we are afraid that something isn't going to work out like we want or expect it to. Adults worry about their jobs, paying the bills, staying well, and other grown-up things. But kids worry too. You might worry about grades, tests, making new friends, or not doing well in sports. Let's face it: we all have plenty of things to worry about!

But the Bible makes it clear that God doesn't want us to worry. When we worry, it tells God that we don't trust Him to work it out. It's natural for us to think about things like tests, schoolwork, and friends and to have some concern for them. If we didn't think about those things, we wouldn't work hard to do a good job. But we don't need to worry so much that we get sick or feel bad about it. God wants you to know that He is in control and that He will help you get through anything that worries you. He knows your past, your present, and your future! He's got it under control!

Dear God, thank You for always being there for me. Help me to trust You more and to turn my worries over to You. In Jesus' name, Amen.

DUCK Commander in ACTION

Here's an experiment you can do to see if trust and worry go together. You will need some cooking oil, a glass, and water. Pour about ½ cup of cooking oil in the glass. The cooking oil represents worry. Now let water represent your trust in God. Pour a little bit of water into the oil. You will see that oil and water don't mix, just like worry and trust in God don't mix. You can't do both, so put your trust in God. He's the One who can help in any situation.

Be Happy for Others

We will shout for joy when you succeed. We will raise a flag in the name of our God.

Psalm 20:5

The word *succeed* means to do well at something. Being successful can mean different things to different people. One person might think he is successful if he is on the gymnastic team. Another person might think she is successful when she makes all A's on her report card or hits a homerun. Adults think they are successful when they have a job they love and can provide for their families. Phil thought he was successful when he sold a million duck calls! And he was!

Yes, success is different for each person. Our job, as friends and family members, is to be happy for the success of others. The Bible gives us an example and tells us to "shout for joy" when someone succeeds. The opposite of being happy for others is called jealousy. Sometimes we look at another person's success and feel jealous or maybe sad because it didn't happen to us. When we feel a little bit of jealousy, we need to *stop* right there and remember to shout for joy instead of being jealous. Jealousy has a nickname—"the green-eyed monster." Don't let the green-eyed monster steal the joy you should have for others. Don't let him be the boss of you. You stand up to that monster, and be happy when others succeed.

Dear God, help me to be happy when those around me succeed and to be happy with what I have and what I am doing. Thank You for all the ways You have blessed me. In Jesus' name, Amen.

DUCK Commander in ACTION

Jealously is no fun for anyone. It makes you and those around you sad. Remember that life is rarely fair. Everyone lives a different life, and what happens to others won't necessarily happen to you. But God will give you exactly what you need if you depend on Him.

If you have been jealous for some reason, write it down, and go bury that paper in the yard. You don't want your life to be ruled by jealousy. You want to live a life that shouts for joy for everyone!

Say No!

And now he can help those who are tempted. He is able to help because he himself suffered and was tempted.

Hebrews 2:18

Temptation is a big word that means being asked to do something you know is not right. Temptation happens to everyone. Even Jesus was tempted. Did you know that? Being tempted isn't the problem, and it isn't a sin. Temptation is what happens *before* sin. The temptation to sin comes first; then, if we do the thing we are tempted with, it's a sin. For example, when Uncle Si was in the army, he was tempted to say bad words because everyone around him said bad words. But Uncle Si knew better, and he worked hard to keep his words clean. When you are at school, you might be tempted in the same way. Kids might want you to say bad words or be mean to another kid. It might seem hard to resist a temptation, but God has some good news for you. He sent His only Son to earth to live as a human so He could understand your temptations and help you overcome them. Jesus knows that you will be tempted, but He also knows you can stand up against those temptations and do the right thing. Learning to say "no" to temptations will help you live your life without drama. And nobody wants drama!

Dear God, thank You for being with me and helping me stay strong. I want to lead others by my example and to stay away when others tempt me to do wrong.
In Jesus' name, Amen.

Take Care of YOU

I praise you because you made me in an amazing and wonderful way. What you have done is wonderful. I know this very well.
Psalm 139:14

When God created you, He made you special. No one is just like you. Your height, hair color, eye color, and personality were hand-picked just for *you*! One way to tell God that you are thankful for your body is to take care of it. One time Uncle Si was feeling bad, so he went to the hospital. He found out his heart needed an operation to fix it. At first he didn't want to do it, but the doctor said he had to because his heart wasn't strong anymore. So Uncle Si agreed to the operation. Now Uncle Si is back to hunting and fishing and doing all the things he loves to do.

There are things you can do to keep your body healthy. You can eat your fruits and veggies. Even if you think you don't like veggies, you need to eat them because they are good for you. Another thing you can do is get plenty of exercise. Run and play every day for at least thirty minutes. And you can drink plenty of water. These are simple ways to show God that you are thankful for the body He gave you.

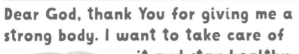

Dear God, thank You for giving me a strong body. I want to take care of it and stay healthy. Help me to make good choices. In Jesus' name, Amen.

DUCK Commander in ACTION

On a piece of paper, trace your handprint. Write these words in the middle of the hand: *I am fearfully and wonderfully made.* Cut out your handprint, and put it on the refrigerator to remind you to eat healthy foods and get plenty of exercise.

Jesus Stays the Same

Jesus Christ is the same yesterday, today, and forever.
Hebrews 13:8

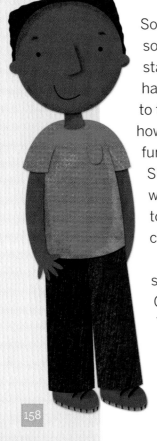

Sometimes we get excited about a change, and sometimes change makes us sad. It's fun to start a new school year with a new teacher; it's harder if you have moved to a new city. It's fun to travel to another country, but it's hard to learn how to eat different foods. Yes, change can be fun, but it can also be challenging. When Uncle Si moved his family back to Louisiana, his wife wasn't sure she would like it. She thought it was too hot, and the food was too spicy. It was a change she had to get used to.

Life is like that. It's full of changes. But here's some great news. The Bible tells us that Jesus Christ is the same yesterday, today, and forever. That means we can always know what to expect from Him. It's kind of nice when some things don't change. Like when you come home from school and know just where your mom is, or

when you go to church and know exactly where your family will sit. Things that stay the same help us feel safe and secure. Because Jesus never changes, you can always feel safe and secure with Him.

Dear God, thank You for sending Jesus to walk this earth just like we are doing now. Thank You for showing me through Jesus that Your love, care, and protection never change. In His name, Amen.

Throw Away the Bad

God has great mercy, and because of
his mercy, he gave us a new life.
1 Peter 1:3

Miss Kay has many stories about food because she loves to cook.
Her kitchen always smells good, and she loves to invite friends over
to eat. But when she and Phil were first married, there was a time
when her kitchen smelled awful! Phil had caught a wild hog and
brought it home to cook for dinner. It turned out
the hog was a boar hog and not good for eating,
but Phil thought if he boiled it long enough, it
would be okay. Miss Kay says her kitchen has
never smelled so bad. She had to throw away
the hog—and the pot too! Yuck!

When we do things that are wrong, God does
not throw us away, but He does throw away our
sins and lets us start over like a shiny, new pot.
It's up to us to see when we need to throw a bad
thing away and start over. You might be arguing
with your brothers and sisters, or you might be
disobeying your parents. God says those things
bring a bad "smell" to your family life, and you
need to throw them away. In God's great mercy,
He will let you do that and start a new life.

Dear God, thank You for letting me start over every day. Help me to see when I need to throw away the bad and start again with the new. In Jesus' name, Amen.

DUCK Commander in ACTION

If your mom has a candle with a sweet smell, ask her to light it and sit down where you can smell it. Read the verse for today, and think about how God loves to let us start over and smell clean again. Say the prayer below, and enjoy some quiet time with God.

God Looks Out for Us

He guards those who are
fair to others. He protects
those who are loyal to him.
Proverbs 2:8

Korie and Willie were excited to get to live in
Italy as part of their college education. Living in
a foreign country can have its scary moments.
One time, they were taking a train to Barcelona,
Spain. While going through the south of France,
a group of thieves got on their train. Willie slept
with his feet on the door so he would know if
the thieves tried to open it. Later that night he
fell asleep, and the thieves stole their friend's
backpack. Willie chased the robbers
until they dropped the backpack. He
took the backpack to his friend,
but he didn't sleep the rest of the
night! He was too busy looking
out for their safety.

That is just how God is. He
is always watching over those
who love Him. The Bible tells us

He guards us. Do you have a guard dog? Guard dogs know their owners and are responsible for their safety. There are many stories of dogs who have rescued children from swimming pools and from being lost in the woods. God is so much bigger and better than a guard dog. He is always watching out for us.

Dear God, thank You for always watching over us. You protect me, and I am safe with You. Help me to depend on You and not be afraid. In Jesus' name, Amen.

DUCK Commander in ACTION

There is a song called "I Am a Sheep." You may have heard it. The first lines are about how we are sheep and the Lord is our Shepherd. It goes on to say, "He is constantly watching over me." Look up this song online with an adult, and read all the words. It is a great reminder of how God watches over us and guards us.

Controlling Anger

When you are angry, do not sin. And
do not go on being angry all day.
Ephesians 4:26

Being angry happens to everyone. Even God gets angry when someone does something against Him. The problem isn't the anger; it's how you handle the anger. According to this verse in Ephesians, we are not to let our anger cause us to sin, and we're not supposed to stay angry all day. Phil and Miss Kay make it a rule in their marriage to not go to bed at night angry with each other. Since they have been married for more than fifty years, it must be a good idea.

But how do you handle your anger when kids at school or on the playground do wrong things to you? For one thing, you can stop focusing on your problems. The longer you think about what happened to you, the madder you will get. If you choose to focus on God, the anger will start to go away. Letting anger grow inside you will allow it to get so big that the anger will pop out of you like the air out of a big balloon. But if you let the anger go away slowly, you will feel better and won't blow up.

Dear God, help me to control my anger. Help me to call on You when I feel like I'm getting angry. Thank You for giving me a way to stay calm. In Jesus' name, Amen.

DUCK Commander in ACTION

If you have a balloon, blow it up as big as you can, so you can see what anger can do when you let it fill you up. Then slo-o-o-o-o-wly let the air out. When you focus on God, you can release that anger to Him. This will make everyone happy, happy, happy!

Be Fair

Then your goodness will shine
like the sun. Your fairness will
shine like the noonday sun.
Psalm 37:6

It would be nice if everything in life was fair, but life doesn't work that way—because what seems fair to one person doesn't seem fair to another. You might complain to your mother that she treats your younger brother or sister in a way that seems unfair. Willie and his brothers used to complain that Jep got everything he wanted because he was the baby. Of course, it wasn't true, but it seemed true to his older brothers.

Most of the time we think something isn't fair just because we want things to be our way.

As you get older, what you think is fair will change, but it will still be based on your opinion.

Being fair is rarely fair! Does that make sense? Remember, what seems fair to one person might not seem fair to another. So what can you do about it? You can work on being as fair as *you* can be. You can always play by the rules; you can take turns and share; you can listen to others; and you can be careful not to blame others when something goes wrong. This way *you* are doing your part to keep things fair.

Dear God, thank You for being a fair God. Help me to treat others fairly and always to be kind. In Jesus' name, Amen.

DUCK Commander in ACTION

Look at these four things, and decide if they are fair. You might want to discuss these with a grown-up.

1. You take the last piece of pizza.
2. Everyone on the basketball team gets to try to score.
3. You let someone get in front of you in line.
4. You only share with kids who have blue eyes.

167

God's Miracles

God does wonderful things that people
cannot understand. He does so many
miracles they cannot be counted.
Job 9:10

When Korie was a little girl, her Papaw Howard loved to cook fish
for her. He loved to hear her say, "More fish, Papaw, more fish!"
There's a story in the Bible where the apostles (the followers of
Jesus) had to ask God for more fish. Have you read it? It's found in
Mark 6. This story is different than Korie's fish story because this
story is about a miracle. Miracles are supernatural—things humans
can't do—and show the power of God. If Papaw Howard wanted to
get Korie more fish, he had to go to the lake and catch them. But in
this Bible story, Jesus had only two small fish and was able to feed
five thousand men with them. Now that's a miracle!

There are many great lessons in this story, but an important one
is that your problems are never too small for God. On the day that
miracle happened, someone probably thought, *What can Jesus do
with just two fish?* But God can do anything He wants! Don't ever be
afraid to ask God anything. Just like Korie's Papaw wanted to give
her more fish, God wants to give you what you want and need. So
ask God . . . and then expect a miracle!

Dear God, thank You for the gift of miracles and for always working in my life. Help me to see what You do each day and to be thankful. In Jesus' name, Amen.

DUCK
Commander
in ACTION

Read the story of Jesus feeding the five thousand in Mark 6. Then take a piece of construction paper, and draw a fish. You can color it or decorate it and then cut it out. Write this Scripture on it: "With God's power working in us, God can do much, much more than anything we can ask or think of" (Ephesians 3:20). Tape it to your bedroom door as a reminder.

Sing Praises

Sing to him. Sing praises
to him. Tell about all the
wonderful things he has done.
1 Chronicles 16:9

The Robertson family loves to sing. Recently little Mia has joined her mom, Missy, singing around the country. Mia tells her story of being born with a cleft lip and palate. That means the top of her mouth wasn't formed correctly when she was born. She has had many surgeries for doctors to fix it. Recently she had a big surgery and couldn't eat for more than two months! She had to drink all of her meals. But Mia has been so brave and has made everyone so proud. Through all of her hard times, she has encouraged others and praised God.

Now Mia is traveling around the world, telling others about God's love for her. She does this by speaking and by singing. The Bible tells us that singing is a way to praise God. Singing praises to God honors Him and makes Him happy.

When you are in Bible class or at a worship service, open your mouth and *sing*! Don't worry that you might not have the best singing voice. God doesn't worry about it! Every sound you make brings Him joy. As long as you are singing with a happy heart, God is being praised.

Dear God, thank You for the gift of singing. I want to use my voice to sing praises to You and to bring joy to others. In Jesus' name, Amen.

Look up Psalm 47:6. Count the number of times it says to sing praises in this one verse. It's a lot! Singing must be very important to God. What is your favorite church song? Ask everyone in your house what their favorite worship song is. Write them down, and the next time your family sits down for some family time, *sing*!

God Is Patient with Us

You will produce fruit in every good work
and grow in the knowledge of God.
Colossians 1:10

When each of the Robertson men got married, Miss Kay would give their new wives cast-iron pots to cook with. Then she has each new wife over to her kitchen, and she teaches them how to make her husband's favorite recipes. The wives were all young and very new cooks when they got married, so Miss Kay had to be patient with them as they learned how to cook. Aren't you happy when someone is patient with you? Think about your teachers at school. Every person learns at a different pace. Some pick up math easily, and for some it takes time. Teachers have to be patient with all their students.

God is just like a good teacher or Miss Kay. He is patient with us and lets us grow at different paces. Growing in God means learning more about Him so we can act like Him. Plants grow things like apples, figs, and oranges. But when we grow, we grow things like more joy on tough days, stronger love for each other, and kindness for everyone. You might still need to grow in some areas—everyone does—but God is patient, and He knows you will get there.

Dear God, thank You for being patient with me. Help me to grow in all the ways You want me to grow. In Jesus' name, Amen.

DUCK Commander in ACTION

Patience is being willing to wait for something good to happen. Watching a plant grow is a great way to learn about patience. Go to the store, and buy some seeds. Plant that seed and water it every day. Write down how long it takes for it to start growing. When you water your plant, remember that God is watching over you just like you are watching over your plant.

Be Generous to Others

A generous person will be
blessed because he shares
his food with the poor.

Proverbs 22:9

Willie has a pond in his backyard. One day he decided he wanted to make the pond bigger and deeper. He hired a man with a big truck to dig out the hole. He dug and dug. Soon the pond was bigger, but now there was a big pile of dirt beside Willie's house. The man had to find another place for all the extra dirt. He came back to the house and moved the dirt to some land that needed to be higher. He found a good spot for the extra dirt.

Have you ever cleaned your room by throwing all the toys in the closet? Then your closet is a mess! In America, we have so many blessings. In fact, most of us have *too much* stuff. It just piles up until we don't even know what we have. But there are people all over the world who don't have plenty of stuff. They don't even have *enough* stuff. You can help those people. The Bible tells us to be aware of those who need help and to be generous. *Generous* means to give freely and happily to others. When you see that you have too much stuff, think about how you can help someone else who needs it.

Dear God, thank You for blessing me with more than I need. Help me to be aware of others who need help and to give when I can. In His name, Amen.

The Best Gift Ever!

"For God loved the world so much that
he gave his only Son. God gave us his
Son so that whoever believes in him may
not be lost, but have eternal life."

John 3:16

Miss Kay loves Christmas! She decorates her whole house and gets her boys to put up hundreds of bright, shiny lights. On Christmas Day, the family gathers up for a Cajun Christmas with fried shrimp and fried meat pies. Then they all crowd into Miss Kay's small living room to open presents. If you didn't know the family, you would think it was totally unorganized. But to them, it is normal. There is lots of laughing and loud talking and wrapping paper being thrown everywhere.

One of Miss Kay's traditions is to give silly gifts. She shops all year for the perfect silly gift to make everyone laugh and have fun. Getting gifts *is* fun. Can you think of your favorite gift? Maybe it was at Christmas or on your birthday. Did you know that many years ago, God gave you the best gift ever? That's right. God gave all of us the gift of His Son, Jesus Christ. He allowed Jesus to come to this earth so we could have an example for living.

Jesus Christ came to earth and lived just like we live. Then He died on the cross for our sins. *That* is the best gift ever!

Dear God, thank You for sending Your Son to earth for *me*. Thank you for seeing that all people need a Savior and for the sacrifice You made for us. In Jesus' name, Amen.

DUCK Commander in ACTION

Getting gifts is fun, but giving gifts is fun too. God loved giving Jesus to His people. He gave Jesus because of His love for us. When you love someone, you want to bless them. Look around your room for a gift you could surprise someone with. When you find something, wrap it up and give it to them. They will be so happy that you thought about them.

The Power of God

I want to see this because the kingdom of God is not talk but power.

1 Corinthians 4:20

John Luke has a boat. It's actually a sailboat, so John Luke has to wait for windy days to go sailing. If there is no wind, the boat won't go anywhere. It will just sit in one spot. But on a windy day, John Luke flies across the lake! He loves his boat and takes great care of it. It's a beautiful boat, white with bright blue sails. When it glides across the water, everyone stops to watch. As much as John Luke loves how pretty his boat is, he knows that the real power behind his boat is the wind.

We are just like a sailboat. God wants us to take good care of ourselves, and He loves who we are and how He created us, but our real power lies in Him, not us. When we look to God to power us, He will make great things happen. He will give us strength and courage. He will help us sing praises and tell others about Jesus. He will be our "wind" and will take us to many great places.

Dear God, thank You for being my strength. Help me to know that all I am comes from You. In Jesus' name, Amen.

To see how powerful wind is, fill up a sink with water. Now put an empty plastic water bottle in the water. Watch how it stays still once you have let it go. Now blow gently on the bottle. It will start to move across the water. That's what the power of God will do for you.

God's Mirror

A person who hears God's teaching and does nothing is like a man looking in a mirror. He sees his face, then goes away and quickly forgets what he looked like.
James 1:23-24

Do you look in a mirror every day? You probably do. What happens when you look in a mirror? You probably make some changes!

Perhaps you notice that your hair needs brushing or your shirt is buttoned wrong. We look in a mirror for one purpose—to see what we look like and then to decide what needs to be fixed. One day, Willie looked in the mirror and noticed his hair was too long. It's always long, but on that day, Willie decided it was too long, so he went to the barber and got a haircut.

In the book of James, it says that if a person hears about God, but doesn't change his life, it's like a man looking in the mirror and then forgetting what he looked like. That would be silly, wouldn't it? If we look in a mirror, we remember what we saw. Seeing ourselves helps us know what we need to do. That's called *a call to action*. We should do something because of what we saw. When we hear God's Word, it should be another call to action. It should cause us to do something for Him.

Dear God, thank You for Your Word. Help me to read it and apply it to my life every day. In Jesus' name, Amen.

DUCK Commander in ACTION

Try this experiment: look at yourself in the mirror, but *don't* change anything. If your hair is messed up, don't touch it. If you have something on your face, don't clean it. Just walk away. This will probably make you feel strange. You won't get far before you want to look in the mirror again. Then you'll want to fix those messes! Treat God's Word the same way—read it and then *do* what it says.

Do Good Everywhere

When we have the opportunity to
help anyone, we should do it.
Galatians 6:10

The Robertsons travel each year to the Dominican Republic to work with the children at an orphanage. Many times they bring them new clothes, which is something they need. Other times they take them to get ice cream. This isn't something they need, but it makes them happy. Sometimes people just need someone to encourage them and show them that they love them. This is what the Robertsons do for the children in the Dominican Republic.

It's a long way to the Dominican, and the Robertsons know that not everyone can go so far away from home to help others. The good news is you don't have to travel very far to help people.

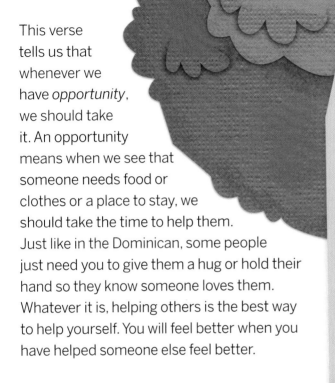

This verse tells us that whenever we have *opportunity*, we should take it. An opportunity means when we see that someone needs food or clothes or a place to stay, we should take the time to help them. Just like in the Dominican, some people just need you to give them a hug or hold their hand so they know someone loves them. Whatever it is, helping others is the best way to help yourself. You will feel better when you have helped someone else feel better.

Dear God, thank You for the times when You have sent others to help me. Help me to see what I can do for others and then to do it. In Jesus' name, Amen.

DUCK Commander in ACTION

You should have plenty of opportunities to help others as you live each day. The problem is that we don't always see the opportunities. Take time today to look for opportunities to help others. At the end of the day, tell your parents all the ways you helped others. This will help you see that God puts people in our path for us to help. We just have to look for them.

Heaven Is Our Home

But our homeland is in heaven, and we
are waiting for our Savior, the Lord
Jesus Christ, to come from heaven.
Philippians 3:20

Home should be our favorite place. It's where our family lives. It's the place where we can rest and get away from the busy things we do in life. Most of the Robertsons live on the same street. It's fun for them to be able to walk next door and see their cousins. They don't have to worry about cranky neighbors because their neighbors are all their family members. They don't have to lock their doors during the day because everyone is welcome to come in their houses. Sometimes they all eat together and watch *Duck Dynasty*.

The Robertsons love being together on the same street, but they know that this is not their real home. They know that heaven is their real home and that it will be even better than the street they live on now. God has prepared a house for you too. Heaven will be everything good at one time. We don't know everything about heaven, but we do know that all of God's family will live there. Surely heaven will be full of the sweetest sounds and the happiest people you could ever imagine. It will be the best street *ever* to live on!

Dear God, thank You for heaven. Thank You for getting it ready for me so one day I can live there with You. In Jesus' name, Amen.

DUCK Commander in ACTION

Get a blanket and go outside so you can look up at the heavens. As you're lying on the blanket, imagine life in heaven. Think about who you might see and what you might say. Close your eyes and sing a song to God. "Jesus Loves Me" would be a great song to sing because He does. He loves you so much that He is getting a home ready for you.

The Best Letter

He loves the Lord's teachings.
He thinks about those
teachings day and night.
Psalm 1:2

When was the last time you wrote a letter? Maybe you've never written a letter because today we just talk to each other with our cell phones. We can call or text our friends and family easily with our phones, so there's no reason to write a letter. One summer, John Luke decided it was time to write letters again, so he wrote a letter to a friend and the friend wrote him back. Soon several of John Luke's friends were writing letters.

Before telephones were invented, writing letters was the only way to communicate. Even God used letter writing to talk to His people. God's letter is the Bible. The Bible is written to all of us, mostly to tell us that God loves us. It also tells us how to live a good life, how to obey God, and how we can get to heaven. The Bible is an important letter. If you got a letter in the mail, you would probably open it as soon as you got it. God wants you to be excited to open His letter too. He wants you to read it daily and learn from it.

Dear God, thank You for the Bible. Thank You for knowing that we all need help to get through each day. Help me to open my Bible daily to read Your Word. In Jesus' name, Amen.

DUCK Commander in ACTION

Ask your mom or dad to help you write a letter. You might want to write your grandparents or a friend who lives far away. Be sure to tell that person that you love him or her and what you have been doing lately. Always remember that God's letter, the Bible, is the most important letter you will ever get.

Love Is Number One

Hatred stirs up trouble. But
love forgives all wrong.

Proverbs 10:12

All of the granddaughters love to cook with Miss Kay. They take turns stirring the bowl that contains things like eggs and flour and milk. If they are making chocolate chip cookies, they have to stir in chocolate chips. To *stir* means to blend or mix something together. When we are cooking, our goal is to stir the right things together to make something yummy.

But the Bible talks about another kind of stirring that isn't good. That's when we use our words or actions to "stir up" trouble. Sometimes this happens because we don't like someone, or maybe someone is doing something that bothers us. Maybe someone in your class is bossy or says unkind things to you, so you are tempted to be mean back. But the Bible warns us that being mean back is not the answer. That would be stirring up trouble. How we act toward others is one thing, but the Bible also tells us not to have feelings of hate. And that is something we can control. It might not be easy, but it can be done. If we start to feel hate toward someone, we can pray about it and God will help us to change the way we think.

Dear God, I don't want to be someone who stirs up trouble. I want others to want to be around me and to see that I treat others with love and kindness. Help me to be the kind of person You designed me to be. In His name, Amen.

DUCK Commander in ACTION

It's a good day to cook! Maybe you can make a cake or some cookies with your family. Today, while you're cooking, think about stirring good things together in your life *and* in your bowl. If your recipe calls for eggs, you can think about eggs being kindness. If your recipe needs milk, milk can stand for patience. Making your dessert today will result in a yummy snack and a better *you!*

Listen to Advice

Listen to advice and accept
correction. Then in the
end you will be wise.

Proverbs 19:20

Sometimes we don't like the word *discipline,* or *correction*, because we think that correction only happens when we are in trouble. But discipline and correction simply train us to behave a certain way. You've seen a baby cry out at church, and it seems normal. But what if you saw a teenager act that way at church? That would be strange, wouldn't it? That's because a baby hasn't learned how to act in church, but a teenager has learned and knows not to holler in church.

The Robertson men are thankful that Phil taught them how to behave. They didn't always like the discipline he gave them, but they now know it was for their own good. They are good men today because Phil loved them enough to correct them. When you aren't behaving like God wants you to behave, your parents are there to help you remember the best way to act. As you get older, your parents won't have to remind you as much. You will be able to correct yourself. That will make God very happy!

Dear God, thank You for putting people in my life who love me and want the best for me. Help me to listen to them and accept what they say to me. In Jesus' name, Amen.

DUCK Commander in ACTION

The Bible tells us that wisdom comes from listening to advice. Get a piece of paper and a pencil, and ask the adults around you to give you some advice. Write down their advice, and put a date on it so you'll remember the good advice you got from people who love you.

Be Strong

But David said to him, "You come to me using a sword, a large spear and a small spear. But I come to you in the name of the Lord of heaven's army."

1 Samuel 17:45

When Will was in preschool, his playground was covered in tiny rocks. The teachers wouldn't let Will pick up the rocks and throw them because they knew a rock might hurt another child. It was very hard for Will to play on that playground and leave the rocks on the ground, but his teachers were right. In certain hands, even a tiny rock can be a weapon.

There's a great story in the Bible about a little boy who defeated a giant with only a rock. The young man's name was David, and the giant's name was Goliath. Goliath's people, the Philistines, had attacked God's people, the Israelites. Over and over, Goliath had made fun of the Israelites, saying that they could never defeat him. But David knew that only one person could defeat Goliath and the Philistines, and that person was God.

So David picked up a stone, put it in his sling, and threw it at the giant. And the giant fell to the ground dead! David was only a small boy with a small stone, but God gave him the power to defeat his enemy. God will give you the power to defeat your enemies too.

Dear God, thank You for helping me be strong when I don't feel very strong. You helped David, and I know You will help me too. Give me strength and courage. In Jesus' name, Amen.

DUCK Commander in ACTION

Your enemy probably won't be a giant named Goliath. But there will be times when you need to be stronger than you think you can be, and God will be there for you just like He was with David. Goliath was nine feet tall. Ask your mom or dad to help you measure off and mark nine feet on a wall or on the floor. Then measure how tall you are. David's enemy was big, but God is bigger!

Remember Your Teachings

Always remember what you have been taught. Don't let go of it. Keep safe all that you have learned. It is the most important thing to your life.

Proverbs 4:13

Sadie can spin a basketball on one finger. It's not an easy trick, but with practice anyone can do it. One day Sadie watched an older basketball player spinning a basketball on one finger. She was fascinated by the trick. So Sadie asked this older player to show her how he did it. She went home and remembered exactly what the basketball player had said. She spent hours working on the trick, and soon she could do the trick as well as her friend.

In the Bible we are warned not to forget something that is much more important than a basketball trick. God wants us never to forget His teachings. When you go to Bible school or when you read the Bible, God doesn't want

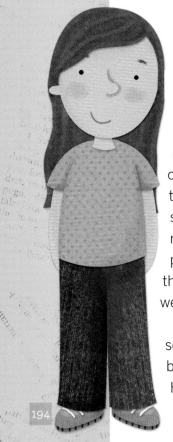

you to walk away and forget what you heard. No, He wants you to keep what you learned in your heart and head. The Bible instructs us to keep God's Word safe. That means to lock it away in our head just like we would a favorite toy or some money. If it's locked away in our head and heart, then when we need it, it will be right there to help us. If you can keep God's Word spinning in your head, you will be able to conquer anything!

Dear God, thank You for giving me Your words to help me make it through each day. Help me to remember everything I've been taught and to keep it safe in my heart. In Jesus' name, Amen.

God Hears Us

I call to you, God, and you answer me.
Listen to me now. Hear what I say.
Psalm 17:6

John Luke was like all toddlers and loved to call his mommy over and over again. In fact, one day, he said *mommy* so many times that Korie finally said, "John Luke, do not say *mommy* one more time!"

John Luke stared at her in disbelief and then quietly said, "Korie." Korie had to laugh because John Luke had figured out a way to call her without saying the word *mommy*. After all, she didn't say not to call her name!

Here's the great thing about God. You can say His name over and over, and He will never get tired of hearing it. In fact, He loves for you to call His name. Calling someone by name says to that person that he or she is important to you. Sometimes moms or teachers can get tired of kids calling their name, but they really do love it. It tells them that they are important people to their children. Never be afraid to call on God. He will always be ready to listen to you.

Dear God, thank You for always being here for me, for letting me call You over and over again, and for not getting tired of me. I love You! In Jesus' name, Amen.

DUCK Commander in ACTION

Today everyone has a cell phone. People use cell phones to call friends, cousins, grandparents, or anyone else. But that isn't how we call God! To call God, we don't need anything. We can just think it, and it will happen. And everyone can call Him at the same time. Isn't that cool? No waiting! Talking to God can sound like a prayer, or it can sound like you're just talking to a friend. Why not have a conversation with God right now? Just tell Him about your day!

197

Listen to God

Samuel said, "Speak Lord. I am
your servant, and I am listening."
1 Samuel 3:10

When the guys go hunting, they dress in camo and paint their faces so they will blend in with the trees in the woods. Then they have to stay very quiet and listen for any sounds of animals coming near them. Listening seems like one of those easy jobs in life, but it can actually be very hard. Because if we want to really listen, we have to be *really* quiet and patient. And most of us want to talk instead of listen. Right?

Samuel is a Bible character who can teach us a lot about how to live our life for God. Samuel wanted to know what God wanted him to do, so the Bible tells us he called out to God and told God that he was listening. Today, listening to God might mean to listen to His Word as a teacher tells you about Jesus. It could also mean reading God's Word yourself. Or it might mean to listen to your parents and other adults in your life who are there to help you. God's voice can also be heard in other people we meet or just by looking at His creation all around us. God is speaking to us if we will just listen.

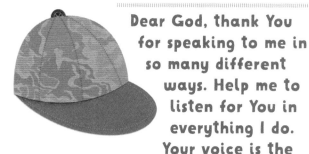

Dear God, thank You for speaking to me in so many different ways. Help me to listen for You in everything I do. Your voice is the voice I want to hear the loudest. In Jesus' name, Amen.

DUCK Commander in ACTION

Hearing God might be something we need to practice. Find a pencil and some paper, and go outside to hear sounds of God. You might hear a bird sing or a baby cry. Write down all the sounds of God you hear. Then pray for each one.

Wisdom from God

"This lesson comes from the Lord of heaven's armies. He gives wonderful advice. He is very wise."

Isaiah 28:29

Do you know what the word *wise* means? You might think *wise* is the same as *old*. Most people think that older people are wiser than younger people. It's true that as we get older, we have more experiences and we learn from those experiences. But someone who is young can be wise too, because wisdom is more about making good decisions than it is about being old.

Every decision we make is better when we take our time and use wisdom to make it. Your parents have had be wise when deciding things like where your family lives or what job they do. When Uncle Si got out of the army, he had many decisions to make. He wasn't sure what he should do. So he prayed to God to help him make good decisions. The Bible tells us that God gives the best advice because He loves us and wants the best for us. God will send people our way with good advice. He also has messages for us in the Bible that help us make wise decisions. If you are facing a tough decision, be sure to ask God to help you with it.

Dear God, thank You for putting people in my life to guide me. Even though I am young, I want to make wise decisions each day. In His name, Amen.

DUCK Commander in ACTION

The Bible tells us that wisdom comes from God. Here are three wise things to remember: 1. God is there to help you. 2. God's Word is where you can find answers. 3. God's people are here to guide you. See if you can think of one thing that would be wise to share with others.

A Strong Foundation

"Everyone who hears these things I say and obeys them is like a wise man. The wise man built his house on rock."

Matthew 7:24

Korie and Willie built a new house right behind their old house. It was fun for the family to watch the house be built. Each day something new was added. But the first thing that the builders had to do was pour a foundation. A foundation is the base of the house. It's what makes a house stay strong and not collapse. In Louisiana, most houses have a foundation made out of concrete or cement. The carpenters carefully lay down boards in the shape of the house and then they pour concrete into the boards. Once the concrete dries, the house will be built on that hard foundation.

When we choose to follow Jesus, hearing His words and obeying them will help us build a strong foundation for life. A strong foundation for a house protects the house against a storm; a strong foundation with Jesus will protect us from the storms of life. Storms of life might be sickness, or losing something or someone important to us, or having trouble with a friend. If we have a foundation built on Jesus, those storms will not knock us down.

Dear God, thank You for giving me words to keep me strong when tough times happen. Thank You for being a strong and mighty foundation for my life. In Jesus' name, Amen.

DUCK Commander in ACTION

It's easy to see how valuable a strong foundation is. Line up four paper cups touching each other. Then put three cups on top of those four. Then two on top of the three. And then one on top. That one cup on the top is able to stay there because of the strength of the four on the bottom.

A New Start

The Lord's love never ends. His mercies
never stop. They are new every morning.
Lamentations 3:22-23

If you have ever cooked for a Robertson man, you know they don't do "leftovers." Maybe your mom makes leftovers from the meal you had the day before. For example, if you had ham for Sunday lunch, you might have ham sandwiches for lunch the next day. Using leftovers is actually a smart way to plan for meals, even if the Robertson men are picky about it!

Guess who else doesn't do leftovers? God doesn't! Does that mean God doesn't eat the same thing twice? Probably not. The Bible doesn't really tell us about what God eats. But this is not about food; this is about His love for us. The Bible tells us that God's love for us is new every morning. If you made a mistake yesterday, once you ask for forgiveness, God doesn't even remember it. As long as you are looking to God, He looks at you as a new creation each day. There is nothing about you that is leftover or left out in God's love for you.

Dear God, thank You for loving me so much that You forget all my mistakes and let me start over each day. Help me to always show my love for You and to make wise choices. In Jesus' name, Amen.

DUCK Commander in ACTION

It's great to know that God sees us as new creatures every morning. If you have a chalkboard or a dry erase board, draw a picture of yourself on it. Then erase it and draw *you* again. That's how God sees you—brand new each day.

Buckle Up with God

"But those who listen to me will live in safety. They will be safe, without fear of being hurt."

Proverbs 1:33

Recently, the Robertson kids went to an amusement park that had a roller coaster ride. Bella is the youngest child, and she didn't want to ride the roller coaster. But the older kids convinced her that she would be okay, so she finally said yes. Do you think she really was okay? Was it safe for her to ride? Yes, she was safe. What made the ride safe? If you are thinking the ride had a seat belt, then you are right. It had a super-duper seat belt that kept Bella from moving at all! In fact, Bella couldn't get out if she wanted to!

When you think about God, think about how He is like your super-duper seat belt. He wraps His arms around you and keeps you safe. But there is something you

Seat belts are a part of our everyday life. Today, when you put your seat belt on, say the verse from Proverbs 1:33. You could shorten it by saying, "Those who listen to God live in safety." This will be a good reminder that God loves you and wants to protect you, but that you need to listen to Him.

must do. On a roller coaster or in your car, you have to actually buckle up the seat belt. God wants to protect us, but we have free will. *Free will* means we can decide if we want that protection or not. Bella's ride took her on twists and turns, even upside down, but Bella never moved because she chose to wear a super-duper seat belt. Choosing God is making the right choice to keep you super-duper safe.

Dear God, thank You for Your love and protection. Help me to be ready to listen to You and be obedient. In Jesus' name, Amen.

God Is Everywhere

In the beginning God created
the sky and the earth.
Genesis 1:1

Jase Robertson will tell you that his favorite place to be is in the woods. He loves to hear the sounds the wind makes as it blows softly in the trees. He loves to see the different colors God created for each tree and bush and flower. He loves to watch the animals scurry around to their homes in the woods. Being in the woods gives Jase a sense of peace, and he feels close to God in a special way.

God truly created a masterpiece, didn't He? When we look at what God created, we can see God and get to know Him better. Just by looking around, we know that God loves to give His people special treats—a sunset to end our day or a rainbow after a rainstorm. And God must love the color blue! He created a great, big blue sky just for us! Looking around, we also know that God will provide for us. The Bible tells us that even the flowers know this. Yes, creation is a reflection of God. You might not live in the woods or close to the woods, but you can still see God if you look around. Even if you just have a tiny flower in a tiny pot, you can see God!

Dear God, thank You for Your creation! I look around and see Your hand everywhere, and I am blessed. Help me to appreciate it more. In Jesus' name, Amen.

DUCK Commander in ACTION

Unless it's raining, today is a great day to get a blanket and go outside. Don't take a cell phone or an iPad or anything else electronic with you. Lie down on your blanket and look at the clouds. Look at the shapes of the clouds. Can you see one that looks like an elephant? How about a pig? It's fun to see what shapes the clouds make, but mostly it's good to look around and appreciate the world God made. He is everywhere!

Responsibility Rules

Each person must be responsible for himself.

Galatians 6:5

Willie gets teased on the *Duck Dynasty* show because he is the boss. Being the boss means you have to be the responsible one. On the show, the other guys in the warehouse sometimes act silly and don't want to do their work. But in real life, the Robertsons value being responsible. Being responsible means that when you are asked to do something, you do it. Being responsible means doing what needs to be done to take care of yourself and others. Being responsible means others can depend on you.

When Phil invented his duck call, he had to work hard to get it in stores. Once a store said they wanted his duck call, Phil had to be sure their order was filled on time and with the right number of calls they asked for. He made sure every order was filled properly. He was a responsible businessman, as well as a hunter. Today, the business is still run by responsible men and women. Being a responsible person tells others that you think they are important. God calls us to be responsible in our schoolwork, at home, and in our jobs. It's a very important character trait, and it's a choice. Choose to be a responsible person. You will be happier, and so will everyone around you.

Dear God, I want others to be able to trust and depend on me. Help me to be a responsible person and to look for ways to help others. In Jesus' name, Amen.

DUCK Commander in ACTION

Make your own checklist to help you be responsible. Get a piece of paper, and write down a list of five to ten things you need to do every day. Above the list, write the days of the week—Sunday through Saturday. As you do each thing on the list, check it off for the day. Some things you might list are: brush your teeth, do your homework, feed the dog, make your bed, and be nice to your brothers and sisters. Get started! Have fun!

God's Plan for You

"I say this because I know what I have planned for you," says the Lord. "I have good plans for you. I don't plan to hurt you. I plan to give you hope and a good future."

Jeremiah 29:11

Have you ever helped your mom, dad, or grandparents pick berries? The Robertsons love Papaw Phil's homemade jams and jelly. They go perfectly with Miss Kay's homemade biscuits! Yum-yum! But before they can eat, someone has to pick the berries. John Luke is always willing to help. He will spend hours sorting through berry bushes, picking the perfect berry for a delicious jelly.

Did you know that God picked you, just like John Luke picks a berry? It's true. God saw you and determined that you were good and picked you for a special purpose in His earthly kingdom. Yes, He has a special plan for you, and only you can fulfill that plan. No one else has your personality, your abilities, or your gifts. They were created just for you! So what is your purpose? It's hard to know everything you will do in life, but you can know this—God created you to give your life to Him. If you do that, all of your other choices will be easy.

Dear God, thank You for choosing me! I don't know all the plans You have for me, but I know I will keep my eyes open and be ready for anything. In His name, Amen.

DUCK Commander in ACTION

You might not have any berries around your house, but you probably have some jam in your refrigerator. Take a piece of bread and spread some jam on it for a jam sandwich. But this jam sandwich has a special meaning. Let the letters in J.A.M. stand for Jesus Amazes Me! As you eat your sandwich, be amazed that Jesus has a special plan for you.

Battle Ready

So give yourselves to God.
Stand against the devil, and the
devil will run away from you.
James 4:7

Uncle Si served our country for twenty-four years in the army. He was given combat clothes in case our country went to war. He had a gun, a helmet, special boots, a walkie-talkie, and camouflage clothes (that part he liked!). He was also trained in how to use all of his equipment. If he was needed to fight, he was ready!

There's another battle that Uncle Si has always fought, and it also requires special clothes. It's the battle against the Devil. We're all fighting that battle because Satan wants us to leave God and follow him. But God has given us a way to fight Satan. He even equips us with special clothes. They're a little different than the uniform Uncle Si got in the army, but it's the perfect uniform to fight the Devil. First, we will need our belt of truth and our breastplate

Fighting is never good, except when we're fighting against the Devil. The Devil has no power over God's people, so never be afraid to stand up for what is right. See if you can fill in the blanks for the verse today. You can look at the top of the page if you need to. So give yourselves to _____.

Stand against the _____, and the _____ will _____ away from you.

of righteousness. Then our feet need to be equipped and ready to carry the good news of Jesus. Our protection will come from our shield of faith and helmet of salvation. Then the most important part of our battle clothes: the weapon. God provides our sword of the Spirit, which is the Word of God. If you have all of these things, you will be ready to fight the Devil too!

Dear God, thank You for giving me a way to fight the Devil. Help me to be ready for battle and to keep Your Word close to me. In Jesus' name, Amen.

Tell the Truth

So you must stop telling lies. Tell each
other the truth because we all belong
to each other in the same body.

Ephesians 4:25

Uncle Si jokes that 95 percent of his stories are true. Uncle Si does love to tell a good story, but the truth is that Uncle Si is a very honest person and would never intentionally lie. In fact, Uncle Si says, "The naked truth is better than a dressed-up lie."

There's a story in the Bible about two people who were caught lying to God. It's the story of Ananias and Sapphira. They lied to God and said that they had given all their money to the apostles when really they were hiding some. They lied to God, and God was not happy. Our God is a God of truth. Lying is the opposite of who God is; it is who Satan is. And lying never makes a situation better; it makes it worse. When we lie, we feel bad inside, and it's hard to get rid of that feeling. It also causes us to lose the trust

our parents and friends have in us. Once we are caught in a lie, it will take a while for your family and friends to build up their trust again. So always tell the truth—no matter how much trouble you are in. It's the smart choice.

Dear God, help me to be someone others can trust. Help me to always tell the truth and be honest in all that I do. In Jesus' name, Amen.

Facing Peer Pressure

*Do not change yourselves to be
like the people of this world. But
be changed within by a new way
of thinking. Then you will be able
to decide what God wants for you.*

Romans 12:2

Peer pressure might be a new term to you, but it simply means letting your peers, who are the people your age, influence you in a bad way. When we're young, it's easy to let our peers (other kids or our friends) influence us. We might want to be popular with the kids at school or in our neighborhood. One thing the Robertsons learned at a young age is that peer pressure can get you in trouble. The youngest brother, Jep, learned this the hard way when he followed some boys who were not doing the right thing. He disappointed his mom, his dad, himself, and God by the way he acted. Eventually his family did some "family pressure," and Jep saw what he was doing and turned his life around.

Choose your friends carefully. Pick friends who have the same beliefs you have. Choose friends who will help you be a better person. If you have friends who tease you to get you to do something you don't want to do, they are not your friends. It's better to have one or two friends who really care about you than lots of friends who just want to make trouble. When you see others who are doing the wrong thing, walk away, even if they tease you. It doesn't matter. Just keep doing the right thing, and don't let what others say bother you. And don't forget that God is with you!

DUCK Commander in ACTION

Write a note to your best friend, and thank him or her for being your friend. Sometimes we take for granted how special our friends are to us. Let your friends know that they are important to you.

Dear God, thank You for my friends. Help me to be a good influence and not to let others influence me for bad. In Jesus' name, Amen.

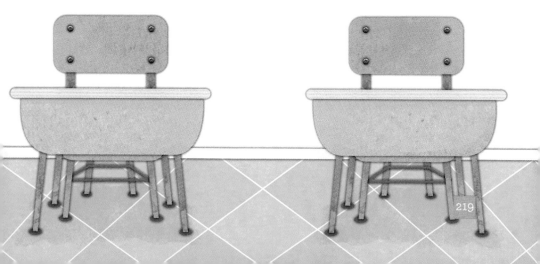

God, Your BFF

Give your worries to the Lord. He will take care
of you. He will never let good people down.

Psalm 55:22

When Sadie was younger, she traveled with a basketball team to Austria. It was a long trip with people she didn't know. The first few days were hard because she felt lonely. Some of the other kids had friends on the trip, but she didn't. She felt left out. All of us will go through times when we feel left out or alone. That can be a very hard time. But that is exactly the time when God loves to show up.

God sees when you are lonely. He knows when you are sad. He understands when other kids ignore you or treat you badly. Did you know that Jesus went through the same thing? The Bible tells us that the people in Jesus' hometown didn't understand Him and didn't accept Him. Everyone wants to be liked and to be a part of the group, but if you are having a hard time, remember that God will never reject you. He loves you and will never let you down.

Dear God, thank You for always being my friend. When other people let me down, You do not. Help me to always know Your love. In Jesus' name, Amen.

DUCK Commander in ACTION

Sometimes we get nervous if we're alone for very long because we get used to people being around us. But it's good to be alone. It gives us a chance to be ourselves with God and to realize that we don't always need someone with us. Find a quiet place outside and sit still for ten minutes. You will see that being alone really means you're with your best friend—God.

A Final Note

We hope you have learned more about God's love for you and His will for your life. We shared stories from the lives of our family members, but you and your family have stories too. Each day, God gives you a blank piece of paper where you can write your life story. Isn't that cool? And you get to start new every day!

Pay attention to how God is working in your life. You will be amazed at His goodness, His grace, and His creativity. Life is like a rollercoaster ride sometimes, but if you keep God at the center of your life, you will be able handle any ups and downs. Thank you for letting us play a small part in your life story by telling you how God has worked in our lives. If you have other questions about God, please talk to your parents, a youth minister, or your pastor. They will be happy to help you.

Hugs and Blessings,

Korie and Chrys

Dear God, You are our hope for a better tomorrow and our comfort for any troubles today. We need You and ask that You guide our steps, guard our hearts, and protect us. In Jesus' name, Amen.